A KILLER

AT THE

DOOR

A KILLER
AT THE
DOOR

A KILLER
AT THE
DOOR

THE DRAMATIC PRISON BREAK
AND MANHUNT FOR
CONVICTED MURDERER DANILO CAVALCANTE

BRUCE E. MOWDAY

SCHIFFER
PUBLISHING

4880 Lower Valley Road • Atglen, PA 19310

Other Schiffer books by the author

Small-Town Cops in the Crosshairs:
The 1972 Sniper Slayings of Policemen William Davis and Richard Posey
978-0-7643-6442-6

J. Howard Wert's Gettysburg: A Collection of Relics from the Civil War Battle
978-0-7643-5391-8

West Chester: Six Walking Tours
978-0-7643-2500-7

ISBN: 978-0-7643-6878-3
Printed in China

Published by Schiffer Publishing, Ltd.
4880 Lower Valley Road
Atglen, PA 19310
Phone: (610) 593-1777; Fax: (610) 593-2002
Email: Info@schifferbooks.com
Web: www.schifferbooks.com

For our complete selection of fine books on this and related subjects, please visit our website at www.schifferbooks.com. You may also write for a free catalog.

Schiffer Publishing's titles are available at special discounts for bulk purchases for sales promotions or premiums. Special editions, including personalized covers, corporate imprints, and excerpts, can be created in large quantities for special needs. For more information, contact the publisher.

We are always looking for people to write books on new and related subjects. If you have an idea for a book, please contact us at proposals@schifferbooks.com.

DEDICATION

Dedicated to everyone diligently working and sacrificing
to keep our communities safe.

CONTENTS

FOREWORD

How did an international murderer wind up loose in our suburban communities for two weeks?

People saw him lurking in their woods. Innocent children waved to him. Dogs announced his presence. Some people mistook him for the neighbor's gardener, never guessing how a casual exchange with this killer would haunt them. Parents rushed home from work only to find their streets barricaded by police while their partners, caregivers, and children were trapped inside homes on lockdown.

No one on his trail was safe for what felt like an eternity, while images of a man who stabbed his girlfriend thirty-seven times in front of her children cut through our nights like a dagger.

It was impossible to sleep. Facebook news feeds gave us the most up-to-date information. Night after night I watched the perimeter of his location move around friends' homes and eventually to my neck of the woods, where he was captured. The twenty-four-hour hum of Homeland Security helicopters amplified the tension.

How could this happen in Chester County, a bucolic landscape graced with fresh air, farms, and forests intersecting with suburbia? Safe, connected communities and exceptional schools drew many of us to this county, the wealthiest per capita county in the state and one of the wealthiest in the nation. We are populated by well-educated professionals, highly skilled laborers, hardworking farmers, business leaders, entrepreneurs, social advocates, and many active faith-based communities. Our police forces are some of the best trained in the nation.

But we were not smart enough to prevent a perfect storm. Starting with a prison guard absorbed in a game on his phone, ignoring a convicted murderer scaling prison walls, a farm van with keys in the visor parked along his escape route, a suburban home stocked with survival supplies, and terrified parents and their children huddled upstairs and a loaded gun poised just inside an open garage door. This story would be hardly plausible if it were fiction.

In reality, it was a debacle of broad interagency negligence. Who better to tell this story than Bruce Mowday, investigative reporter, historian, author of more than twenty-five books and former managing editor of the *Daily Local News*, covering all the initiatives of the Chester County commissioners for the past half century? This saga mirrors *Jailing the Johnston Gang*, a famous Mowday book detailing with precision how a gang terrorized the county and the region for decades. That book includes information on the escape of one of the murderers, Norman Johnston. Johnston eluded law enforcement in the same area as Danilo Cavalcante. Bruce conducted extensive interviews with law enforcement, attorneys, and gang members for his books, including *Stealing Wyeth* and *Small-Town Cops in the Crosshairs: The 1972 Sniper Slayings of Policemen William Davis and Richard Posey*. The book details the first murders by the Johnston Gang.

Here, Mowday's seasoned investigative skills present a disturbing account of events leading up to Cavalcante's escape, the breadth of efforts to capture him, and the resonance of aftershocks among residents. In all, he weaves a tale of loose ends that frayed the nerves of thousands of people, many of whom still suffer from the trauma. Bruce's book on Cavalcante is an exposé of a traumatized community told through multiple interviews and personal accounts.

The trauma of this assault upon our community lives on. Although the threat is over in the external landscape, like PTSD in combat veterans, it lives on in the internal landscape.

There is a silent side to conflict and assault. Through writing our books on history, Bruce's *Lafayette at Brandywine, Pickett's Charge, September 11, 1777, Emotional Brandywine*, and *Emotional Gettysburg*, and my book *Letters to Lida: WWII Told through the Eyes, Heart, and Words of a B-29 Tail Gunner*, we have experienced the vital need for those who suffer the trauma of war to be heard. In response to our book talks, we created a community workshop series for veterans and their families called *The Legacy of War: A Perpetual Assault*. Our workshops provide a forum to share traumatic experiences and facilitate recovery. According to *Trauma and Recovery* author Judith Herman, recovery occurs in three stages: establishment of safety, remembrance and mourning, and reconnection with ordinary life.

The book is a forum to assist with recovery for people whose internal landscape is still on lockdown. It is for people who are still closing their blinds with the memory of a murderer in the backyard, people who cannot go to sleep without lights on, children who still cannot be alone in their rooms at night, and others such as the father who will never forget how his daughter lost something precious the day she innocently waved to a murderer passing through their backyard and how the system failed to help him protect her.

Though the footprints Cavalcante left in our woods have been swept clean by the wind and rain, burning questions linger. How did this happen? What is the lasting impact on individuals in our community? How do we ensure this will never happen again? How do we help those who still suffer?

In true Mowday style, the book eloquently addresses all those questions with no stone left unturned.

Charlene Briggs
May 2024

Charlene Briggs is the owner of Botanical Energetics, a flower essence practice specializing in trauma recovery. She is an environmental scientist and educator promoting ecological restoration and relationship with the land, an author, and former associate adjunct professor at Temple University. For more information, see www. EarthVisionsConsulting.com.

ACKNOWLEDGMENTS

So many residents willingly offered to give their time to describe their experiences during a terrifying two-week period in the summer of 2023 and a long-ago August 1999. I thank everyone who assisted in the writing of this book.

The suggestion to focus on the community came from a friend, former colleague and therapist Michele Paiva. Thank you, Michele, for planting the idea. Another friend, colleague, and therapist, Charlene Briggs, provided a great foreword for this book, chronicled her experiences, and was so supportive during the research and writing of this book.

Of course, the book wouldn't have been possible without the professional team at Schiffer Publishing. Editor Bob Biondi, publisher Peter Schiffer, and Carey Massimini, acquisitions and foreign-rights manager, all backed this project from the beginning. This is our second team book project and my fourth with Schiffer Publishing.

Mary Walsh, a talented editor and author and a good friend, reviewed the manuscript to weed out my errors and offer cogent suggestions. Mary has been an excellent partner on numerous projects. Also helping with the initial development of the manuscript and reviewing the final copy was Simsun Greco. My brother Barry Mowday forwarded to my attention articles he read on the subject.

Usually, when I write a book I don't have close friends and acquaintances I can contact for information. That wasn't true in this book; so many of them assisted. They included Tom Cloud, David Richter, George Asimos, Patty DeFroscia, Laurie Curl, Gayle Sauers, Barry Rabin, Michael P. Rellahan, Bill Quindlen, James Flamminio, Carolyn "Bunny" Welsh, Harry McKinney, Tony Grosso, Jack Crans, Susan Hamley, Steve Plaugher, Fred Fonseca, Vince Pompo, Emilie Bane, Alan Oliver, and Jeff Taylor.

The professionalism of the law enforcement team was mentioned time and again during my interviews. US marshal Steve Eckman emphasized during his interview that the teamwork among all the agencies needs to be commended. Both Steve and Marshal Rob Clark provided excellent details on the search for the murderer. Chester County chief detective David Sassa and then District Attorney Deb Ryan, now a Chester County Court of Common Pleas court judge, were in charge of the initial hunt. They sat for an interview early in the background-gathering phase of this book. West Caln police chief Curt Martinez talked about his part in the search and his K-9 partner's activity. Dr. Bert Schiffer provided information on EMS and the medical services available during the search for Cavalcante. Longwood and Po-Mar-Lin Fire Companies greatly assisted during the search for the murderer. A special thanks goes to Longwood chief A. J. McCarthy, since he sat for an extended interview. FBI agent James Milligan was agreeable to be interviewed. Tina Jagerson, Sofia Kettler, and Allison Weston of the FBI assisted.

I reached out to a number of government representatives for assistance. Former colleague Becky Brain of the Chester County Commissioners Office was a great help, as was then Chester County commissioner Michelle Kichline. Senator Carolyn Comitta and her director of communications, Adam Cirucci, made contacts for me with the Pennsylvania State Police. Stacey Witalec, communications director of the Administrative Office of Pennsylvania Courts, provided legal updates and assisted me with media credentials during Cavalcante's preliminary hearing, as did Chester County court administrator Patricia Norwood-Foden and Constable William Carozzo. Carozzo also was interviewed as he participated in the search.

Unionville–Chadds Ford School District superintendent John Sanville provided excellent background on the effect the search had on the school district and students. His assistant Linda Miller helped schedule the interview, and Chester County Court of Common Pleas judge Patrick Carmody vouched for my credibility with Sanville. Thank you, Judge Carmody. Patricia Evans of Longwood Gardens entertained my questions about the famous gardens. At the Brandywine Museum of Art, chairman of the board Cuyler Walker assisted, as did Nicole Kindbeiter, director of marketing and communications.

Pocopson resident and historian Don McKay receives a special thank-you. Don sat for an interview and then gave me a grand tour of the township that only a native Pocopsonite could provide. Pocopson supervisor Raymond McKay, Don's father, talked with me, and Pocopson supervisor chair Elaine DiMonte spent time answering my questions. McKay suggested I talk with Randy Mims. I spent time interviewing Randy while sitting in his picturesque yard, not far from the prison, about his experiences during the search.

Giving great insight into the excellent precautions taken to keep residents of Kendal-Crosslands communities safe were Lisa Marsilio, CEO; Seth Beaver, vice president; and Michele Berardi, senior director of communications and public relations. Col. Willard C. Conley, US Army (Ret.), and I had a conversation at a talk I gave for the Military Officers Association of America. He then organized a meeting with residents of the Traditions at Longwood community. Those attending were Ed Wyatt, Celeste Scozzafava, Gene Rogers, Tom Detweiler, Tony Musacchio, Kathy Conley, and Will Conley.

So many people consented to be interviewed, including two mother-and-daughter duos. Allison and Kyndal Jacobs talked to me during a book signing at the Exton Barnes & Noble store, and later we did an interview. The same goes for Nancy Brill and Sharon Maxwell. Nancy then put me in touch with her sister and brother-in-law, Amy and Joe Dettore. Amy and Joe had valuable input into this book.

Judy Love, Pocopson's Paul Revere of this story, was a great help in talking about her administration of a Facebook page and identifying community members with Cavalcante experiences.

For sitting for interviews, giving assistance to key people to interview, and offering support, I thank Ryan Dummund, Robert Daull, Linda Bowman, Bruce Norcini, Loraine Lucas, Jim Karustis, Brian Sprowal, Jamie Hicks, Vijay Bhardwaj, Robin Matrippolito,

Kathryn Humpfry, Veronica Horn, Michele Lynch, Dean Ardnell, Cathy Molique, Eric D. Ruggeri, Patrick Meehan, Rich DeRafalo, and Jeff Cantwell.

This book has truly been a community collaboration. Thank you to everyone. I apologize if I missed someone.

INTRODUCTION

A Facebook message arrived the day the massive and intense two-week search for convicted murderer Danilo Cavalcante concluded. Brazilian Cavalcante was cornered and captured in a field in northern Chester County, Pennsylvania, by national, state, and local law enforcement officials, assisted by a K-9 named Yoda.

"Let's write a book on this," the message implored. There was a caveat; I had to be interested in "an emotional take" on the story. "How people reacted to knowing a killer was out there, the emotions and emotional triggers, the emotions of a killer, this would be fantastic," the message concluded.

Her message was clear. The book needed to encompass more than just law enforcement's relentless quest to return a convicted murderer, who is facing another homicide charge in his homeland, to a secure jail cell.

Books tell me to write them. I don't intentionally set out to write many of my books. This work came as a result of that Facebook message. This book has multifaceted dimensions. The hunt, the murderer, law enforcement, the community, fear, traditional media, the huge financial loss, the demise of traditional journalism, new-age social media, bounty hunters, inefficient bureaucracy, and unexplainable human behavior all are intertwined. This is not the work I contemplated when I initially approached Schiffer Publishing in October 2023. This book developed into an internal examination of not only the community surrounding Chester County Prison, but also today's society.

Michele Pavia, a therapist and former colleague at the West Chester newspaper *Daily Local News*, authored the Facebook note. As the days passed, Michele wasn't the only person inquiring if I would write a book on Cavalcante. At my public book appearances and notes received on social media, readers inquired, "Is Cavalcante your next book?" Another reader stated, "You are the natural one to do so."

Previously, I authored three Chester County true-crime books about serial murderers, the sniper-slayings of two Kennett Square policemen, and the theft of millions of dollars of art from the homestead of world-famous artist Andrew Wyeth. The books germinated from criminal cases I covered for the *Daily Local News*. A fourth county true-crime book on Cavalcante seemed natural to many surrounding me. I wasn't so sure.

At first, I wasn't convinced a book on Cavalcante was viable. While Cavalcante was on the loose and terrorizing the community, every move the murderer made and every possible sighing, while valid or not, captured the public's attention. Many were mesmerized by the daily police briefings, news media reports, and the sometimes wildly speculative minute-by-minute reporting of the new social media.

Would interest in Cavalcante and a book on his exploits hold the public's interest after six months? Once the murderer was securely nestled in a state prison and the public was no longer menaced by a murderer on the loose, would his name fade from the collective minds of the public? The public has a short attention span, after all.

Certainly, Michele's suggestion that the book be community centered on the effects of Cavalcante's escape was intriguing. I was sold on the book concept after Charlene Briggs, an author and therapist, told me she believes that community members were suffering from posttraumatic stress disorder (PTSD) because of the Cavalcante escape and search. Charlene and I have presented PTSD topics connected to our individual writings on historical subjects.

Does PTSD exist in the Chester County community surrounding the prison? The question was answered in the positive by an email sent to me by a grandfather of a child in the Unionville–Chadds Ford School District. The grandfather's daughter didn't want to expose her son to remembering the terrifying days when Cavalcante roamed their neighborhood. The incident was "still too raw."

Thus, I won't identify the family. I respect their privacy and applaud their efforts in protecting their son. The grandfather's initial message is important. It read, "My family and I are excited that you have been chosen to write a book on the prisoner escape. We are most interested in the impact on the community that you plan. My daughter, her husband, and her 10-year-old son live in Kennett Square / Unionville. They would like to be sources to describe the terror they faced. My grandson is still very afraid to sleep by himself. When he hears of a prison escape, we all have to help him cope. Many in the Unionville schools can tell similar stories, but you probably know that. Let us know if we can provide any witness for your book."

Indeed, the communiques on the progress of capturing Cavalcante were frightening to many community members. Even more frightening was the lack of progress reported on many of the days. The Chester County government alert notification system didn't serve neighborhood residents. Many people reported never even receiving information from the county. The alerts were directed to those living within a defined search area. If a resident lived just outside the area, the resident didn't receive the information. The public deemed the alert system to be faulty.

No doubt existed that local residents and beyond—national and international news media covered the hunt for Cavalcante—hungered for up-to-date information. Some wanted minute-to-minute updates. When a terrorist attack or disaster takes place across the world, television and larger news organizations provide such coverage. In Chester County, traditional media was decimated long ago by the demise of local newspapers and radio stations. As local ownership disappeared and chain operations sold out to investment firms, reporters were eliminated along with the basic local news coverage of news stories. Early in the twenty-first century, the *Daily Local News* had a cadre of more than twenty full-time reporters and another fifty part-time reporters covering a county with a little fewer than 500,000 people. As the county grew in population, now amounting to more than a half-million residents, the number of reporters supplying local community news and sports decreased to fewer than a dozen.

The nearby Philadelphia media retreated, for the most part, to the confines of the City of Brotherly Love. The *Philadelphia Inquirer*'s West Chester bureau was dismantled years ago. To fulfill their voracious desire for news of the Cavalcante search, many turned to social media and self-styled citizen reporters. The coverage was both helpful and damaging to the public. More than one law enforcement official commented that the social media reporting hindered the police search for Cavalcante.

Those watching live-stream reports often saw law enforcement officers shifting positions and plunging into farm fields and undergrowth in search of Cavalcante. At times, citizens rushed to the scene of the search. What was unknown to the citizen reporters and their followers was the cause of the police action. Were those searches triggered by a deer or other animal or an unverified sighting? Hopes that Cavalcante was finally cornered were dashed time and again as police, in full tactical gear, retraced their steps to a command post at the Po-Mar-Lin Fire Company.

Rumors were rife on social media. Too many of those nontrained reporters didn't attempt to verify information. One blathered on about a "shoot to kill" order being issued. Of course there was no such order. The use of deadly force was allowed, as it always is, if an officer's or a civilian's life is in danger. Shooting first and asking questions later is not part of the Pennsylvania police playbook. Protection of a threatened life is far from a shoot-to-kill authorization. Police complained that valuable time was consumed by nontrained reporters demanding answers to every speculative and outrageous rumor reported.

Some of the rumors were believed to be true by the public. To be sure, many didn't know what source to trust. All they knew for sure was that their daily lives were disrupted, and a murderer was on the loose.

Schools were closed. Pennsylvania State Police officials updated school superintendents twice a day, the first about 4:30 a.m., on the status of the investigation. From that information, school administrators decided if classrooms should be shuttered that day. Businesses were closed, including the world-famous Longwood Gardens and the popular Brandywine Museum of Art. One gas station lost all its business for days as roads were blocked leading to its pumps. While losing income, the owner kept the station open for the use of the investigators. He declined payment for goods consumed by the police and emergency service personnel. He said he wanted to support those keeping his neighbors safe.

Community support for the officers was overwhelming.

Longer commutes to work, school, and shops were necessitated because of the rerouting of traffic. Some departing and returning family members were greeted by armed members of their families. A fear existed that Cavalcante would try to carjack a resident in an effort to escape the search area. The theory was that family members would be most vulnerable entering and exiting their cars.

Indeed, a book examining the effects of a murderer on the loose was warranted. Other elements enhanced the attractiveness of writing this book.

How did Cavalcante escape? Chester County Prison was under close scrutiny in the months leading up to the escape. A study was authorized. The former warden balked at some of the suggested changes and departed his job. And another prisoner escaped just weeks before Cavalcante, by the same method. The day of the escape was the first day on the job for the new, acting warden. Understaffing, outdated procedures, and a derelict correctional officer all contributed to the escape.

Helicopters, airplanes, infrared sensors, the latest tactical gear, and specially trained dogs all were utilized in the search for Cavalcante. With as many as five hundred law enforcement officers taking part in the search, the operation was costly. What were the costs to county, state, and federal taxpayers? The total cost may never be known, but several government officials pegged the cost at $1 million or more a day. Just the overtime for troopers of the Pennsylvania State Police totaled more than $3 million. One public official pegged the total cost in the neighborhood of $20 million, if the loss of business revenue is included.

How did Cavalcante elude detection and capture for so long? The area's terrain is partly the reason. On January 7, 2024, Pocopson resident Don McKay—his family has lived in the area for generations—provided me with a tour of the area where Cavalcante hid for two weeks. Wooded areas, streams, ponds, and thick undergrowth abound in Pocopson.

As McKay, an avid local historian, discussed, Pocopson was part of the Underground Railroad prior to the Civil War. Local Quaker landowners were stops for the fleeing enslaved people. The dense undergrowth and terrain that concealed Cavalcante also hid the slaves.

Another bit of American history took place in Pocopson on September 11, 1777. A portion of the British army under the command of General William Howe outflanked American general George Washington's army during the Battle of Brandywine. Howe's march went through a portion of Pocopson. The terrain shielded the British troops from the eyes of Washington's scouts.

Cavalcante, a diminutive Brazilian, was wanted on a murder charge in his home country. He fled Brazil and made his way to Pennsylvania, entering the country as an illegal alien. His story gained national and international coverage. Despite the brutal murder of his girlfriend and pending murder charge, Cavalcante had some fans rooting for his continued freedom. While the search was taking place, I was told that at least one woman in Chester County commented she wouldn't mind inviting the young murderer into her home.

Some of the equipment utilized was far more advanced than the search for another convicted murderer a quarter decade before in the same community. Cavalcante wasn't the first murderer to terrorize Chester County and the citizens living near Chester County Prison. In 1999, Norman Johnston bolted from a state prison in western Pennsylvania and returned to his roots. Johnston went to Unionville High School and lived in the area of the prison. For three weeks, sightings of Norman took place throughout the county and into Maryland. He was captured traveling toward Delaware, near the burial site of three of his young victims.

Norman Johnston and his brother David were convicted of four murders. The senior brother, Bruce A. Johnston Sr., was convicted of taking part in six murders. Some people believe he killed at least ten. Some locals also supported Norman as he was fleeing authorities and wore "Run Norm Run" shirts.

As for the research and other elements of this book, an explanation is needed. Cavalcante's escape trial was not concluded in Chester County Court before I submitted this manuscript to Schiffer Publishing. Thus, the final trial result is not known. There were plea negotiations discussed. Also, Pennsylvania State Police representatives and judicial officers involved in the escape case weren't available to comment because of the unsettled charges. Pennsylvania government officials investigated the escape, and those results hadn't been released. Not everyone contacted, including elected officials, responded to my requests.

On purpose, I didn't attempt to interview the family of murder victim Deborah Brandao. The family, son, daughter, and sister have been asked enough about the brutal murder. They have testified at court proceedings and talked with numerous reporters. I didn't see any sense in asking them to relive the circumstances of the murder and express their feelings. I also didn't interview Cavalcante and his attorneys, since the trial is still pending. And I didn't take a trip to Brazil.

For this book, I've had interactions with more than eighty people, and most of them were interviewed. I've also consulted court documents and attended town meetings and Cavalcante's preliminary hearing on the murder charges. The book does contain information taken from social media and articles from traditional news outlets. That information is clearly identified in the text. I intentionally didn't interview any of the self-styled social media reporters. Their contributions to the hunt for Cavalcante are noted, both good and bad, in the book.

This book captures the anxiety and fear of a peaceful community as a methodical search for a convicted murder gripped their community.

Bruce E. Mowday
May 2024

CHAPTER 1

CRAB WALKING

Videos and still photographs of a murderer "crab-walking" up a prison wall dominated social media and traditional news outlets around the world for two weeks in the summer of 2023. The escape from a prison in suburban Philadelphia, Pennsylvania, even sparked a "crab-walking" fad of sorts. People were intrigued about the skill needed to scale such a wall. Some visited fitness centers to learn the Ninja Warrior technique.

On a hot summer's morning, just outside the confines of Chester County Prison, residents exercised on a path without so much as a second thought to the criminals within the nearby walls topped with barbed wire. The residents possessed full faith in the prison officials. That faith would be shaken to its core in the next two weeks.

The security felt by the citizens was based, in part, on a fallacy. Many were under the mistaken belief that only prisoners serving sentences for nonviolent crimes, such as driving under the influence and shoplifting, were housed in the county prison. Murderers and other violent criminals were kept in state and federal prisons, they believed. They were wrong. Chester County Prison is, as advertised, a prison, and violent offenders are housed in the county jail.

Just over a slight hill from the prison, the staff and almost three hundred residents of Pocopson Home, the county's long-term health facility, prepared for the upcoming day. For more than six decades—the medical facility opened in 1951 and the prison in 1959—the two county agencies coexisted as next-door neighbors. The patients were deemed safe despite the proximity to the prison yard and its scalable walls.

Pocopson Home is "situated among beautiful rolling hillsides of Chester County," according to a website posting by Chester County government. Those rolling hillsides, along with nearby dairy and horse farms and the abundance of beautiful landscapes, attracted the affluent to Chester County from near and far for decades. During the past half century, the county's population doubled and soared to more than a half million people.

Upscale housing developments, fifty-five-plus communities, and retirement villages occupy portions of the nearby landscape. Additional apartment buildings and housing developments were popping up all over Chester County in the summer of 2023.

Chester County, situated about 30 miles west of Philadelphia, is known as one of the most desirable places to live in the country. At least, a number of national surveys and studies comparing communities attested to the county's desirability. Fine schools, recreational opportunities, and cultural and historical destinations abound in the county. Reported crime was much less in Chester County than in big cities and more-populous areas. That doesn't mean the county was crime-free. The county has its share of violent offenders.

As demanded by a community of means, education must be top notch. The local public school district, Unionville–Chadds Ford, received high marks. On that summer's day in August 2023, students were settling in for a day of classes. Summer vacation recently concluded. The new school year was a few days old.

A leading tourist attraction in the nation is Longwood Gardens, a botanical garden of more than 1,000 acres, located about 2 miles from the prison. Pierre S. du Pont, entrepreneur, businessman, and philanthropist, purchased a farm in 1906 and provided funds for the garden's expansion and upkeep. In 1921, the garden opened to the public. Today more than a million people a year visit the world-famous garden. On that summer's morning, staff members were busily preparing for visitors. Some of those early guests included mothers and fathers with young children strolling the grounds for a morning's walk before the temperature rose uncomfortably high. Chester County was about to experience a heat wave.

The origins of the Brandywine School of Art began along the banks of the Brandywine River in Chadds Ford, just a few miles from the prison. The art movement was nurtured by Howard Pyle and made famous by his pupils, including N. C. Wyeth and Wyeth's son Andrew and grandson Jamie. The Brandywine Museum of Art holds many Wyeth family artworks and attracts artistic aficionados from across the country.

The proprietors of a Karco gas station and convenience store stood ready to attend to morning customers. The Karco station is located just south of the prison and northeast of Longwood Gardens, at the intersection of Routes 926 and 52. After losing a job because of the COVID shutdown and restrictions, Vijay Bhardwaj and his wife, Roop Kumari, opened the franchise.

At Baily's Dairy, located on Meadow Farm, on Lenape Unionville Road, the daily chores were well underway. The owners, fourth generation of the family farm, welcome visitors to view the dairy-farming process and the production of the farm's hormone-free, 100 percent natural milk and dairy products, including ice cream. In recent years, the farm became a favorite venue for children's birthday parties. The farm's location is an easy walk from the prison and close to Longwood Gardens.

The daily routine of those living in the area of the prison and those associated with the businesses and cultural institutions would soon drastically be altered.

Families prepared for the upcoming Labor Day weekend. Trips to the food store were planned to stock up on supplies for barbecues and picnics. Officials at nearby Radley Run Country Club readied the golf course for an upcoming holiday members' tournament.

For the moment, the lives of residents were tranquil and peaceful. For most, nearby Chester County Prison and the criminals housed within were out of sight and out of mind.

Pocopson, the township where the prison is located, and surrounding municipalities in Chester and Delaware Counties are by no means an idyllic paradise. Traffic taxes the road system during rush hours. Many of the byways were developed from paths used by the Lenni-Lenape Native Americans before the land was deemed part of the William Penn land grant. Petty and other minor crimes take place, the same as in any other community in the country. And, occasionally, a violent crime is perpetrated.

Pocopson residents weren't thinking about crime and threats to themselves and their families as they prepared for the 2023 Labor Day weekend. They didn't live in constant fear for their lives, as was the case in some sections of the world, even in nearby Philadelphia.

On Thursday, August 31, 2023, residents went about their morning tasks in the same manner that they performed them on previous summer days.

All was well in Pocopson Township and Chester County.

Inside Chester County Prison, acting warden Howard Holland prepared for his first day on the job. The Chester County commissioners hired Holland, formerly chief of police in the Chester County community of Downingtown, in April 2023 to be their liaison with the prison and then warden Ronald M. Phillips.

Phillips, a longtime prison employee and well-liked administrator by most under his command, was placed on administrative leave on July 28 by the Chester County Prison Board, the ruling body of the county prison. Subsequently, Phillips resigned and retired. The prison board appointed Holland to fill the job, at least on a temporary basis, on August 30, 2023.

The prison, unbeknown to the general public, was plagued by internal issues, many triggered by the recent international COVID epidemic. Phillips and the prison board disagreed on solutions to be taken to solve those prison issues. A lack of prison employees didn't make the administration of the prison easy for Phillips. In February 2023, the prison board summoned an outside agency, the National Institute for Jail Operations, to conduct a "comprehensive evaluation" of the prison's policies, procedures, and overall working conditions. The organization was paid $28,985 by county taxpayers to conduct the assessment. The amount of the contract would be a drop in the proverbial bucket compared to the upcoming costs associated with Chester County Prison and the about-to-happen prison escape.

Before the report was issued by the National Institute for Jail Operations in July 2023, inmate Igor Bolte decided to vacate the prison by crab-walking up a wall in the exercise area. On May 19, 2023, Bolte was quickly recaptured. The prison's escape warning siren was not activated. The community was not informed of Bolte's flight. Pocopson residents later criticized the county government for not alerting them to Bolte's bolt and the possible dangers within the prison walls.

Communication between the government and residents was about to be exacerbated, big time. For the moment during that hot summer's morning early hours, community members continued their peaceful lives without concern.

A daily rhythm takes place in Chester County Prison. Prisoners wake, eat breakfast, and begin their routine for the day. The days can be monotonous for the inmates. The correctional officers need to be vigilant every second of their shifts. Every day the officers are confronted with inmate issues. Some of the problems come from inmates suffering from mental illnesses. Mental issues are the root cause of some prisoners' difficulties. Bolte was described as such an inmate. Correctional officers can't afford to be lulled into a false sense of serenity, even if the prison appears to be calm.

Prisoners receive meals in assigned units. After a morning meal, the prisoners have time to spend in their cells (many have television sets) or in a day room with other prisoners. There are trips to the infirmary, meetings with legal counsel, and opportunities to meet with staff of the prison chaplain. Inmates are guaranteed at least an hour of exercise. The prison is a busy place, and not all the inmates are easily monitored by an undermanned staff.

Thursday, August 31, 2023, began the same as other repetitive days at the prison. By 6:00 a.m., some of the prisoners were beginning to think about eating their morning meal. Correctional officers arrived for the 8:00 a.m. shift and gathered for a meeting where work assignments were distributed for the upcoming day.

Some of the prisoners were playing an early-morning basketball game. Other inmates in the exercise yard were spectators. One of the prisoners on the sidelines was a diminutive Brazilian, Danilo Cavalcante, who had recently been convicted of committing an atrocious and vicious murder. He stabbed his girlfriend thirty-seven times in front of her two children.

So much for the mistaken belief that only nonviolent offenders were housed at the prison. The fact that the prison had a maximum-security section belied the belief that only nonviolent prisoners occupied cells. Violent criminals occupied cells for decades. Cavalcante was an occupant of the maximum-security section of the county prison.

Regulations called for Cavalcante, and other such maximum-security prisoners, to be escorted by a correctional officer when not in their prison cells. On that morning, Cavalcante was accompanied by a correctional officer to the exercise yard. After arriving, the correctional officer made sure the convicted murderer made his way into the exercise area for his mandated time in the fresh air. No other correctional officer patrolled the grounds of the exercise yard with the prisoners. In years gone by, when staffing was less of an issue, multiple correctional officers would have stood watch over the prisoners.

In the summer of 2023, the prison was severely understaffed.

The duty of keeping a keen eye on Cavalcante, who had a history of eluding law enforcement in Brazil and Pennsylvania, and all the other prisoners in the exercise yard switched to a correctional officer in an observation tower.

Cavalcante's route of travel from the holding area to the exercise area was documented by a prison camera. Nine inmates were led into the exercise yard. Leading the parade of prisoners was Cavalcante. Cavalcante was carrying a towel, not typical but not unusual for prisoners entering the yard. A towel would be useful after playing a game of basketball in the hot sun. Also, the towel would be useful in protecting hands while scaling a wall protected by barbed wire.

Acting warden Holland reported that Cavalcante and the rest of the inmates entered the prison's exercise yard precisely at 8:33 a.m. Unlike the other inmates, who were focused on playing a congenial game of basketball before the heat of the day became too intense, escape was on Cavalcante's mind. Cavalcante was aware of Bolte's crab-walking escape three months earlier and the obstacles Bolte faced during his escape, including razor wire. Prison officials had reinforced the wire deterrent after Bolte's escape but had not totally blocked the escape hatch. The additional wire was not a deterrent to Cavalcante.

Prison officials were well aware that Cavalcante was an escape risk. In fact, a correctional officer noted he received information in July that the murderer was planning to abscond from custody. That knowledge had not been forwarded to acting Warden Holland until after Cavalcante demonstrated his crab-walking prowess and fled the confines of Chester County Prison. When questioned after the escape, county officials stated that the information on Cavalcante's expressed desire to escape was not deemed credible. No explanation was given as to why the report was dismissed or who made the determination. Not known are which members of the correctional staff were informed of the potential flight by the convicted murderer.

County elected officials evaded many direct questions concerning the state of the prison before the escape.

Even without the direct knowledge that Cavalcante was intent on fleeing, Cavalcante's record clearly indicated he was a flight risk. Cavalcante fled his native Brazil after being named as a suspect in a murder. He made his way to Puerto Rico and then to Chester County, where a protection-from-abuse order was issued against him. He fled across the commonwealth to Pittsburgh to avoid being served with the legal document. After murdering his girlfriend in front of her two children, Cavalcante again fled before being arrested in Virginia.

Yes, Cavalcante had freedom on his mind on that hot summer's morning in August. Cavalcante, who stood just 5 feet tall and weighed about 120 pounds, surveyed the exercise yard and identified an opportunity to gain freedom.

The prison's video camera recorded Cavalcante and another prisoner at the exercise yard's wall less than twenty minutes after entering. The spot was where Bolte previously fled. The inmate standing near Cavalcante told law enforcement that he was watching a basketball game and not acting as a lookout to assist the convicted murderer in scaling the prison walls.

At 8:51 a.m., just eighteen minutes after Cavalcante entered the exercise yard, the prison's video camera documented him beginning his ascent. Cavalcante placed his hands on one wall and his feet on the other wall. The inmate then shifted weight and shimmied his body upward toward the roof. Since the escape, some have debated what the escape maneuvering should be correctly termed. For sure, the world identified Cavalcante's stylist ascent as "crab walking."

No prison employee was monitoring the institution's camera at the moment Cavalcante made his getaway.

Holland reported that Cavalcante escaped by crab-walking up the prison wall. The prisoner then pushed through some razor wire, ran across a roof, scaled another fence, and pushed his way through more razor wire. Cavalcante jumped into a field and began walking southward along Wawaset Road. In his almost direct path were the Karco gas station, Longwood Gardens, plus-fifty-five retirement communities, other retirement communities, and upscale housing developments. His route took him past Pocopson Home and the community walking trail with unknowing and unsuspecting residents.

Thus, Cavalcante began his two weeks of freedom.

What happened to the correctional officer in the observation tower standing sentry over the exercise yard? Was he on a bathroom break? Did another inmate distract him? Was he a coconspirator of the convicted murderer?

No is the answer to all the above possibilities. On the basis of statements made by a number of persons interviewed for this book, the correctional officer was playing a game on his cell phone. Chester County officials declined to provide detailed information on the dereliction of duty by the correctional officer. The county has a prohibition against disclosing personnel actions against Chester County government employees.

What *was* reported was that the cell-phone game player, an eighteen-year county employee, was fired on September 7, 2023, a week after the escape.

The county government mantra was soon formed: a single point of breakdown—the dereliction of duty by the correctional officer—was solely responsible for the escape. While the game-playing correctional officer might have been the final breakdown in Chester County government's correctional system, a number of elements built upon each other over the years to make Cavalcante's escape possible.

The fired correctional officer wasn't the only person to pay for Cavalcante's flight to temporary freedom. Taxpayers—county, Pennsylvania, and federal—also paid a steep price. Because of all the agencies involved in the subsequent search, the exact total cost hasn't been disclosed and may never be known. Pennsylvania State Police reported more than $3 million was paid just in overtime pay to troopers. Several government officials involved in the search for Cavalcante estimated the law enforcement cost at $13 million; that's $1 million a day. Other government and law enforcement officials said the price estimate of $1 million a day was low. The loss of business added millions more to the cost of the escape.

The total monetary loss was placed in the $20 million range. The loss of trust, security, and personal well-being was dearer.

As many as five hundred law enforcement officers, as noted by police officials, were involved in the search from local, state, and federal agencies. While some were paid regular salaries, some received additional overtime. Some were transported to Chester County from other sections of the country to aid in the search. Some of the troopers drove more than two hours just to reach the search area and begin their shifts. The massing of law enforcement personnel necessitated travel, housing, and food costs. Helicopters were kept in the air constantly, and planes with infrared capabilities were utilized. The bill for the helicopters started as soon as the rotor blades began revving. The costs of material, transportation, and other resources added to the taxpayers' bill.

The taxpayer cost doesn't account for the money lost by Longwood Gardens, the Brandywine Museum of Art, the Karco gas station, and other businesses and organizations.

When asked about Chester County taxpayers' portion of the bill, the county's response was "Regarding the cost incurred by Chester County Government of the Cavalcante manhunt—there was no specific accounting performed of the costs to the County for the Cavalcante search. All expenditures were covered by existing 2023 budget allocations, resulting in no financial impact to County taxpayers." The county didn't detail what portion of the cost applied to the county. "The County does not have details of costs incurred by other law enforcement agencies and how those costs have been covered, so cannot comment or speculate on them."

The price for Cavalcante's escape was dear even if Chester County government officials wouldn't put a price tag on the operation.

CHAPTER 2

CHESTER COUNTY PRISON

"How does anyone escape from a prison?"

Elaine DiMonte, chair of the Pocopson Township Supervisors, asked the question as Chester County officials prepared for the first of many press conferences during the two weeks following the escape of Danilo Cavalcante.

In the township meeting room was Josh Maxwell, a Chester County commissioner and chair of the Chester County Prison Board. Another man preparing to meet the media was unknown to DiMonte. Maxwell turned to DiMonte's mystery man and commented to DiMonte, "Why don't you ask him? He's the acting warden."

During the first part of September, DiMonte, acting warden Howard Holland, and Maxwell became well acquainted as the hunt continued for the escaped murderer causing havoc with the residents DiMonte represented.

Despite the claim by Holland and others in Chester County government that the cell-phone-playing derelict correctional officer was the sole cause of a dangerous murderer roaming the county's suburban landscape, a number of problems, known to government officials, contributed to Cavalcante's escape.

The state of security for the prison and the whole county's justice system was a cause for concern before August 31, 2023. In fact, Chester County Court employees discussed the subject the very day before Cavalcante absconded. A member of that discussion group recalled they all wondered when a major security breach would take place. The court employees knew it would be only a matter of time. The exact time was the next day. The cracks in security at the county's prison, sheriff's office, and justice center were myriad.

How the prison was administered by then warden Ron Phillips became a focal point of the county's prison board and commissioners months before Cavalcante escaped. The prison board consisted of Chester County commissioners Marian D. Moskowitz, Josh Maxwell, and Michelle Kichline; the Court of Common Pleas president, Judge John Hall; district attorney Deb Ryan; Sheriff Fredda Maddox; and controller Margaret Reif.

Those criticisms began before 2023. Phillips's management style was in question, according to former commissioner and prison board member Kichline. She and other prison board members wouldn't comment on the exact details of the complaints. County officials cited the prohibition against disclosing personnel matters involving employees, the same rule quoted when declining additional information on the fired employee. Phillips declined to be interviewed for this book.

Those who worked with Phillips at the prison and knew him from his part-time employment in the security department at Longwood Gardens liked him, for the most part. Phillips was described as a hands-off administrator who readily delegated authority. The lack of direct control was a concern for his bosses on the prison board.

Those concerns spurred the Chester County commissioners to approve a contract in February 2023 with the National Institute for Jail Operations. The organization was to provide training and a "comprehensive evaluation" of the prison's policies and procedures and overall working conditions.

The findings of the taxpayer-funded evaluation have not been made public. When documents were requested, the Chester County Solicitor's Office responded that the report may compromise security at the prison.

Maxwell commented on the hiring of the National Institute for Jail Operations during a prison board meeting on September 20, 2023, which was after Cavalcante's capture. According to Maxwell,

from September of 2022, the Chester County Prison Board began noting concerns about the leadership and operations at Chester County Prison and agreed to take action to address those concerns.

One of the actions the prison board took was to bring in a third party to evaluate conditions at the prison—including staff morale and the safety and security of staff and inmates—and report back to the board with their findings. That third party was the National Institute for Jail Operations (NIJO), and a contract with NIJO was approved on February 8, 2023, at a commissioners' public meeting.

In anticipation of the results of the NIJO evaluation, the prison board also decided to hire Howard Holland to serve as a special advisor to the prison board. Mr. Holland began serving as special advisor in April 2023, and he was tasked with ensuring that, based on the NIJO evaluation, meaningful change would take place.

The hiring of NIJO and Holland as special advisor caused more friction between the prison board and Phillips. With his years of experience at the prison, Phillips contended that he knew more about the running of a prison than a nonprofit organization and Holland, a police officer with no correctional experience. In the days during the escape and following Cavalcante's capture, Holland's lack of correctional experience was noted by numerous members of the public at meetings and on social media.

A vast difference exists between a law enforcement official on the street and a correctional officer, according to prison experts interviewed for this book. "On the street, when a disturbance takes place a police officer can retreat a few blocks, call in assistance, and set up a perimeter to contain the problem. In a prison, if you encounter an inmate insurrection, the area is locked down and doors are secured and won't be opened until the threat is under control. The correctional officer remains with the inmates in the locked area," said John Freas, former Chester County correctional officer and officer with the county's sheriff's office. Freas had additional experience as a correctional officer in Montgomery County.

"When a correctional officer enters the prison, the officer is as much a prisoner as the inmates," Freas stated. "Your job is to keep order in the institution. When a situation gets out of hand, you are in there with the prisoners. When I was at Chester County Prison, we had [two blocks] in the chow hall, and we had three or four officers locked in the hall with them. One time an inmate asked me, 'Hey, Freas, what would you do if the inmates took over the dining hall?' I told him I'd try to regain control, but there would not be much I could do with all those inmates." Freas would suffer whatever punishment the inmates wanted to inflict upon him. Freas realized that his fellow correctional officers in the control room weren't going to open the door, even if his life was threatened.

According to a posted job description, Chester County was seeking more of an administrator than a person with prison experience. The stated duties of the special advisor included being "responsible for overseeing the implementation of recommended corrective actions within the Chester County Prison in coordination with correctional consultants/experts, monitoring and evaluating the effectiveness of those corrective actions to bring about the desired change." The job posting continued, "The goal is to improve morale; increase staffing levels to ensure the safety and security of staff and inmates; improve staff retention rates; and operate a high-performing twenty-first-century correctional facility which provides an environment most suited for rehabilitation of those incarcerated."

The prison board didn't have to look far to find its special advisor. Holland, police chief in the Chester County borough of Downingtown, had applied for the vacant Chester County position of director of emergency services before the prison's special-advisor position was posted. The emergency services job went to Bill Messerschmidt. Holland, according to Kichline, passed all the background checks for the emergency services job and came with excellent references. Commissioner Maxwell knew Downingtown police chief Holland, since Maxwell was mayor of Downingtown before being elected a county commissioner.

The three commissioners—Maxwell, Kichline, and Moskowitz—decided a wide search wasn't needed for the prison position, since they had a qualified person at hand. Holland accepted the job offer as special advisor to the commissioners.

As part of the NIJO's research, an on-site, unannounced three-day evaluation took place. NIJO wanted an up-close-and-personal experience. The final report of the NIJO focused on what was believed to be the root cause of prison concerns, which was the leadership within the prison administration.

When the report was issued, Phillips was placed on administrative leave, and then he announced his retirement from his job, which paid him a yearly salary of $137,968. Phillips's relationship with the county commissioners during his last days on the job as warden was much different than the greeting he received when he was appointed warden in October 2020. At the time, Chester County commissioners issued a press release touting the hiring of Phillips. "[Phillips] has nearly 38 years of experience in corrections, including 25 years in leadership roles with Chester County Prison. Phillips served as the deputy warden of treatment, managing the county prison's reentry program, helping inmates who are re-entering the community have access to key programs that will ensure their success. Phillips also served as the director of inmate services for nine years."

At the prison board's August 30, 2023, meeting—the same day judicial employees discussed the inevitability of a safety catastrophe—Holland was appointed acting warden.

Holland, as the job description stated, was instructed to "improve staff morale, increase staffing levels, improve staff retention rates, ensure the facility complied with applicable state and federal laws especially as it relates to the care of inmates, and operate a high-performing twenty-first-century correctional facility."

Chester County Prison wasn't close to being "a high-performing twenty-first-century correctional facility." Holland commented at a public meeting that when he took over the running of the prison, he felt "stuck in 1981." That is, the prison was about a half century behind the times, in Holland's estimation.

The prison that Holland was about to command was extremely busy. Warden Phillips reported to the prison board on June 29, 2023, just two months before Cavalcante's escape, that the average daily inmate population in May was 684, an increase of thirty-eight inmates from the previous year. On May 31, the prison was populated with 711 inmates. Of the inmates, 145 were serving county prison sentences, six were serving state sentences, 329 inmates were awaiting court appearances, and 119 hadn't appeared for preliminary hearings.

In maximum security, where Cavalcante was being housed, thirty-four inmates were contained. Inmates on suicide watch were 11 percent of the population, approximately seventy persons.

Another segment of the inmate population, those with mental illness, caused additional issues and tasks for correctional officers and prison management. Phillips reported that 263 inmates were taking psychotropic medications and that sixty-eight prisoners—fifty-two male and sixteen female—were considered seriously mentally ill. "A psychiatric or psychotropic medication" is defined as "a psychoactive drug taken to exert an effect on the chemical makeup of the brain and nervous system. Thus, these medications are used to treat mental illnesses." Phillips reported that thirteen inmates were housed at Norristown State Hospital, a facility treating those with mental illness. Another inmate was awaiting a bed at Norristown.

Besides the mental issues, by no means were the inmates of Chester County Prison healthy in May 2023. Prisoners attending sick call numbered 489, while 351 inmates were taking over-the-counter medications.

Phillips was operating the prison, which also functioned as a treatment facility for the mentally ill, with fifty-one staff vacancies during the month of May. Phillips reported to the prison board that seven new recruits were scheduled to begin employment.

The chronic understaffing put a strain on all areas of security at the prison. Obviously, Pocopson residents weren't as secure as they believed.

One procedure, if such a procedure is even defined, and its application in the Cavalcante case are unexplained. What happens when correctional officers become aware of a planned escape? Who is informed? How is the information vetted?

Prison officials knew that Cavalcante was an escape risk, and he was planning a breakout. A correctional officer, identified as Hernandez, noted to superiors in July that Cavalcante had freedom on his mind. The source of the information was not disclosed. Hernandez could have overheard a conversation, or a jailhouse snitch could have provided the intelligence.

Chester County public-information officer Rebecca Brain disclosed, "During the time surrounding [Cavalcante's murder] trial, unsubstantiated information from an unknown source was received reinforcing Cavalcante's status as an escape risk." Brain didn't disclose what, if any, steps were taken to verify the information and how the information was deemed to be "unsubstantiated." Brain added, "Chester County Prison's security measures for an inmate identified as an 'escape risk' were enacted and heightened only when the inmate was being transported off prison property." Thus, inmates plotting to break out of the prison didn't receive extra scrutiny.

At some point, Sergeant Jerry Beavers of the prison staff became aware of Cavalcante's escape intentions. Beavers then communicated his knowledge to Captain Harry Griswold.

ABC News obtained emails between prison officials after filing a "right-to-know" request with Chester County government. Soon after Cavalcante's escape was known, Beavers wrote Griswold, "I am just sending this because I don't want this to come back on us or Hernandez in any way. . . . He noted back in July that this inmate was planning an escape."

Griswold then informed Holland. "I am not sure how you want me to move forward with this information internally," Griswold wrote. Thus, Holland was told of Cavalcante's skedaddling intentions postescape.

As evidenced by his crab-walking technique, Cavalcante incorporated lessons learned from inmate Igor Vidra Bolte's earlier escape from Chester County Prison. Actually, Bolte twice breached court-ordered confinement.

The first time was in July 2019 when Bolte was serving a three-month sentence for assaulting a West Chester police officer. Bolte was assigned to the prison's Work Release Center, a minimum-security facility for nonviolent offenders. Without permission, Bolte walked away from the center and ignored an order to stop issued by a correctional officer. Bolte made his way to the woods on South Wawaset Road, a road later used by Cavalcante.

Bolte's freedom lasted a little more than three hours. State police, members of the Chester County Sheriff's Office, and prison personnel searched and found Bolte on Wawaset Farm Lane. Bolte was returned to prison and charged with escape.

On May 19, 2023, just three months before Cavalcante escaped, Bolte again made a dash for freedom. While in the exercise yard at about 6:20 a.m., Bolte crab-walked up the wall and ran across the roof of the prison. The lone correctional officer was distracted by an argument among other inmates in the yard. He turned in time to see an individual in an orange jumpsuit, Bolte, running toward a field near the main entrance of the prison on Wawaset Road.

Bolte's second taste of illicit freedom lasted about five minutes, since he was quickly recaptured. An affidavit filed by Chester County detective Keith Cowdright noted Bolte's description of his escape. Cowdright wrote that Bolte said he (Bolte) "was an experienced rock climber, [and] he was able to climb the walls of the exercise yard with his feet on one wall and his hands on the other, horizontal to the ground. Once at the top, he pulled himself onto the roof and ran across the top until he scaled down a wall near the visitor's entrance, where there was less security."

Bolte's escape was Cavalcante's blueprint. The crab-walking move was popular in the summer of 2023 by inmates. The maneuver was used by a murder suspect, Michael Burham, held in a Warren County jail, to escape in July.

After Bolte's escape, Chester County Prison officials attempted to deter future escapes by placing additional razor wire on the roof. The measure wasn't nearly enough to dissuade, or stop, Cavalcante.

Chester County should have taken additional action to guard against another escape through a weak point in security, according to Freas. "More than a camera and some extra wires were needed," the former correctional officer said. "Wire can only do so much." A correctional officer should have been stationed at the location where the escapes took place until a permanent fix was in place, according to Freas. He added that inmates needed to be kept from that location.

Bill LaTorre, a retired Pennsylvania State Police sergeant who now runs his own security consulting firm, told ABC News that he wasn't surprised Cavalcante was suspected of using the same escape method as Bolte. He was surprised that officials didn't do more to "defeat that strategy to escape."

One correctional officer in the tower couldn't effectively monitor all prisoners in the exercise yards, according to Freas. He said, "When I was a correctional officer in the late 1980s and early 1990s, there were two of us in the yard. Let's face it, the tower officer can only do so much. He is constantly scanning different areas. If he swivels his head to the left, he can't see what is taking place to the right and vice versa."

Outdated procedures, compliance issues, and sick and mentally ill patients weren't the only concerns compromising the public's safety at the prison. A lack of properly trained and paid correctional officers was a constant problem for prison administration, especially during and after the COVID epidemic.

"COVID changed everything," one county prison official said. "Before COVID, Chester County Prison was one of the best in the country. COVID caused a loss of correctional officers through retirement. Many others quit."

Complying with all the county's Health Department COVID directives put an added strain on the prison staff. "The warden [Phillips] made sure all were followed, including wearing of the masks. The mask mandate was not a favorite and made doing duties more difficult when in the prison," one prison employee commented.

Being a correctional officer is dangerous work that requires specialized training. The pay, even before COVID, wasn't high enough to entice the needed professionals to work at Chester County Prison. In Pennsylvania, the reported average hourly pay is less than $25.00. The starting pay for a correctional officer was noted as a little less than the average in the commonwealth. Salaries for members of the sheriff's office are on a par with that of county correctional officers.

On August 4, less than a month before Cavalcante's escape, Brain reported seventy-six vacancies existed at the prison out of 301 total positions. Of those vacancies, fifty-five were for correctional officers.

At the time of the escape, Holland reported that only 60 percent of his correctional officers' positions were filled. The acting warden informed the public in September that there were forty-three openings for correctional officers. Recruitment advertisements for employees were planned for billboards in Chester County.

In addition to struggling to keep the prison operating and tending to the mentally ill with greatly reduced staff, the Chester County Prison administration lost focus on an essential part of its stated mission; assisting inmates to return to society without preying on law-abiding citizens and avoiding a return trip to prison.

On the wall a mission message is printed: "The mission of the Chester County Prison is to ensure the public, as well as the correctional staff, a safe environment that provides detention, rehabilitative, recidivism risk reduction, and re-entry services to those who are incarcerated so that they may live in a clean, humane, and secure environment and re-enter the community as a productive citizen."

To some working within the prison's walls, one section, "rehabilitative, recidivism risk reduction, and re-entry services to those who are incarcerated so that they may live in a clean, humane, and secure environment and re-enter the community as a productive citizen," was being ignored.

Claire Shubik-Richards, executive director of the Pennsylvania Prison Society, was surprised by the cutback in aid to prisoners. She was quoted in a West Chester *Daily Local News* article as saying, "In most facilities, a staffing crisis of this magnitude degrades the health, safety, and dignity of staff and people in custody—meals are served late[,] leaving confined people hungry, [and] delays in accessing medical care leave confined people sick and in pain. Programming is almost always stopped. The security of staff and inmates can be placed at risk. There is no quick fix to a problem the size of Chester County's."

By not paying attention to the practical and spiritual needs of the inmates, opportunities are lost to better our society, a society being ravaged by crime, a lack of universal compassion, and the loss of essential faith. As one prison official said, "The prison should be inspiring inmates, not warehousing them."

For sure, when Cavalcante made his escape, he had no intention of making society a better place to live. He just didn't want to spend the rest of his life being warehoused.

CHAPTER 3

MURDERER

In a matter of hours, Danilo Cavalcante went from an unknown illegal-immigrant murderer housed in a suburban Philadelphia prison, to an international criminal worthy of articles on the BBC, many other international news organizations, and major national news outlets. Daily updates were announced to the world of the Brazilian's successful efforts to evade capture. In Brazil, a Rio de Janeiro newspaper published an extended article with the headline "Dangerous Hide-and-Seek."

Even after his gruesome murder of his girlfriend in Schuylkill Township, near the Chester County borough of Phoenixville, few in the region recognized Cavalcante's name before his escape. The press coverage of Cavalcante's trial and sentencing just weeks before the escape didn't penetrate the consciousness of the local population.

"We don't follow what is going on in Phoenixville; that's the other end of the county," said Joe Dettore, who lives with his wife, Amy, and their six children in Pennsbury Township, just a few miles from the prison and about 20 miles from Phoenixville.

Indeed, editors at the *Daily Local News*, the primary newspaper of Chester County for more than a century, once considered the county to have four different and distinct readerships. Atglen, on the western fringes of the county, was a foreign place to those living in Phoenixville. Philadelphia's Main Line, on the eastern boundary, and Oxford, in the far southern end of Chester County, were estranged. Each quadrant, for the most part, paid scant attention to the happenings in the other segments of the county.

For the *Daily Local News*, covering the whole of Chester County (measuring 759 square miles) and its nearly half-million population and seventy-three different municipalities, it had been difficult with a news staff of more than seventy-five during the late 1990s and early in this century. Since then, the paper, as had many local newspapers in the nation, was sold to a capital investment firm. The staff size shrunk, and local articles offered to its readers dwindled.

When Cavalcante crab-walked to freedom, only a few reporters were stationed in the whole of Chester County. The *Daily Local News* newspaper building was sold after fifty years of use and razed, and the property was converted into an expensive and cramped townhouse development. The editorial staff was anchored in another county. Vital news on the happenings at meetings of school boards, county and local governments, and the courtrooms, once a staple of the newspaper's coverage, was scarcely reported.

The county's major radio station, supplying news for decades, was sold years before Cavalcante's escape, and the *Philadelphia Inquirer* had long since closed its suburban office and relocated its stable of reporters. Only an occasional Chester County news article appeared in the big-city paper. The lack of professionally trained reporters caused a number of headaches for law enforcement in the coming weeks as rumors and falsehoods were disseminated through social media sites, including YouTube and Facebook, as the search dragged on for days. Sadly, the new pseudo media was the only minute-by-minute source of information—not verified facts, for sure—for frightened residents.

Downingtown attorney and newspaper columnist Barry Rabin posted on Facebook, "It's been interesting following the escape and eventual capture of the convicted murderer, Danilo Cavalcante, here in Chester County over the past few days. One of the takeaways I have found is this: Neither the remaining local radio station nor what little remains of the *Daily Local News* (which is now homeless after the private equity fund that bought them sold off the building) have the personnel or resources to be on top of this huge story. If it hadn't been for "the cable news" networks or the Philly TV news teams, we would have had almost no idea what was happening in our own backyard. I know I sound 'old' for saying this, but we were much better off in terms of local news & info 30+ years ago than we are today!"

Amy Dettore, Joe's wife, is in the real estate business. When the prison was mentioned, clients were told that the prison had no effect on the community. Now she wonders if home values will be affected by the Cavalcante story. "We didn't know who was being held at the prison," Amy said. "We were told only prisoners who committed minor offenses served sentences there."

Cavalcante's crimes were major, not minor.

Cavalcante was convicted of first-degree murder and was serving a life imprisonment term at the time of his escape. Also, Cavalcante was wanted in connection with a murder in his homeland of Brazil. As Cavalcante is wont to do, he fled police after being sought by law enforcement officials in South America.

Pennsylvania judicial records state that Danilo Souza Cavalcante was born on July 3, 1989. The records list an alias of Danelo Souza Cavalcante, and many of the news stories spell his name Danelo and not Danilo.

Cavalcante's race is listed as "white," and "his hair black and eyes brown." The diminutive murderer stood 5 feet tall and weighed 120 pounds at the time of his escape. Law enforcement reported he had bushy hair and an unshaven face when he climbed the walls of Chester County Prison.

Pocopson Township, where the Chester County prison is located, is a long way, about 3,700 miles, from the murderer's listed hometown of Estreito, located in the state of Maranhão in northeastern Brazil.

By all accounts, Cavalcante's early life was difficult and disadvantaged. Retired Philadelphia educator Robert Klewans, who once was a teacher in Chester County's Coatesville School District, commented that by his observation as an educator, a poor early homelife greatly contributes to a person taking an antisocial path in life. Cavalcante traveled that path.

Cavalcante grew up poor in Brazil and had been a victim of abuse himself, according to Chester County assistant public defender Sameer Barkawi. The attorney made the comment during Cavalcante's murder conviction sentencing before Chester County Court of Common Pleas judge Patrick Carmody. Barkawi agreed with Klewans by saying, "Those individuals often go on to perpetrate the same crimes they witnessed."

Iracema Cavalcante, the murderer's mother, told a reporter for the *New York Times* that her son abandoned his schooling to work to help support his family. Cavalcante was five years old when he began his employment. She didn't mention what job her son fulfilled. Often, Cavalcante didn't have proper nourishment. "It was going to sleep hungry; it was waking up as I wondered what to feed them," Iracema Cavalcante commented. Cavalcante's father was an alcoholic, Chester County law enforcement reported.

Membership in a street gang and a proclivity for drugs and alcohol sealed Cavalcante's fate as a criminal. Brazilian officials reported that Cavalcante had several brushes with the law as a youth.

One of Cavalcante's friends in Brazil was Valter Júnior Moreira dos Reis, a twenty-year-old student. Cavalcante completed repairs on a vehicle owned by Reis. Cavalcante believed that his friend hadn't fully paid him for the repair work. Cavalcante confronted Reis outside a restaurant in the city of Figueiropolis, Tocantins, Brazil, on November 5, 2017. Both men were reported to be frequent diners at the eating establishment Espeto Lanches.

The debt wasn't settled to Cavalcante's liking, and Cavalcante reportedly fired five shots from close range at his friend. Reis died. "I thought it was fireworks. It never crossed my mind it was gunfire," Evaldo Alvis Faitusa, owner of Espeto Lanches, told a reporter. "It was only when one of my employees ran back inside and said, 'That guy killed his friend.' I couldn't believe it until I went outside and saw for myself."

A week after the murder, the Brazilian public prosecutor's office reported that an arrest warrant was issued for Cavalcante. The murder suspect fled. Fugitive Cavalcante hid in a wooded area to prevent his capture and arrest, Brazilian law enforcement noted. When on the loose in Chester County, Cavalcante chose dense woods and underbrush surrounding the county prison to conceal himself from pursuers. While there is no evidence that Cavalcante was a "trained survivalist" as then Chester County district attorney and now Chester County Court of Common Pleas judge Deb Ryan stated, there is evidence that Cavalcante was experienced eluding police in densely wooded terrain.

After several weeks successfully evading Brazilian authorities, Cavalcante believed the time had come to depart his home country. Cavalcante's escape was aided by lax paperwork by Brazilian law enforcement. Brazilian representatives reported that officials of the Tocantins justice system failed to have the arrest warrant documentation entered into the country's National Warrant Registry until June 2018, seven months after the murder and long after he had fled the country. Brazilian regional district attorney Rafael Alamy confirmed the delay to a Philadelphia television reporter.

Cavalcante was long gone from Brazil by the time the Brazilian arrest warrant was processed.

In January 2018, the fugitive was able to hop a plane at the Brasilia International Airport and fly to Puerto Rico. In Puerto Rico, Cavalcante obtained a fake identification, believed to be a driver's license, and began the second leg of his journey to Pennsylvania and his eventual incarceration at the Chester County Prison. US marshal Steve Eckman stated he was told that Cavalcante took a ship from Puerto Rico to Newark, New Jersey.

The Port Newark-Elizabeth Marine Terminal is part of the Port of New York and New Jersey, and for the most part it is the principal container ship destination for goods entering and leaving the New York metropolitan area. Several cruise lines also utilize the ports within the system.

No information has been obtained about Cavalcante's voyage.

Cavalcante had a United States destination in mind. His sister Eleni Cavalcante and her family lived in a suburban Philadelphia community in Montgomery County. The area has a Brazilian conclave. Eleni entered the United States on a travel visa, which had expired by the time her brother escaped. Her significant other, sometimes described as a husband and other times as a boyfriend, according to federal officials, is a valid resident of the United States. Danilo Cavalcante had no such valid visa and eluded detection by the United States Immigration and Customs Enforcement agency.

Within a year of arriving in the United States, Cavalcante met Brazilian Deborah Brandao. They were from the same area of Brazil, according to Ryan. The two were neighbors for about eighteen months. Cavalcante and Brandao began dating, and a serious relationship developed between the couple. The young mother of two children, daughter Yasmin and son Yan, allowed Cavalcante to move into her Royersford apartment.

Sarah Brandao, Deborah Brandao's sister, told a reporter that early in the relationship, Cavalcante was kind toward her sister and her children. Sarah Brandao said her sister came to the United States because she wanted to give her children a better life than they could experience in Brazil. Cavalcante then changed. Sarah said her sister told her that Cavalcante was "extremely jealous" and "became a different person" when he drank. Cavalcante accused Brandao of seeing other men, an allegation that district attorney Ryan said was untrue.

In June 2020, according to court records, a confrontation between the couple became physical. Cavalcante bit Brandao on her lip. Brandao fled their shared apartment. Ryan and Chester County chief detective David Sassa said they believed not all the violence against Brandao was reported to law enforcement. Ryan said emails attesting to the abusive relationship between the two were obtained but not allowed to be introduced during Cavalcante's murder trial.

Brandao went to Upper Providence police to inform them of the June 2020 assault. Royersford is located in Montgomery County, next to Chester County. Thus, Chester County law enforcement wasn't involved in the assault case. Upper Providence police issued an arrest warrant for Cavalcante but were unable to locate him.

Brandao broke off her relationship with Cavalcante, but Cavalcante wasn't through with Brandao. In December 2020, Cavalcante threatened Brandao with a knife. Again, Brandao sought protection from law enforcement. A protection-from-abuse order was issued against Cavalcante.

There was no way that Cavalcante wanted police to find him and serve the court order. In doing so, law enforcement just might discover he was wanted for murder in Brazil. His freedom thus would end. Cavalcante fled, not to the Pennsylvania woodland but to Pittsburgh, located across the commonwealth of Pennsylvania from Chester County. Cavalcante had friends in Pittsburgh, and they welcomed him.

"He was gifted in eluding police," Ryan commented.

After a period, Cavalcante made his way back toward Philadelphia and was living in the suburb of King of Prussia. Cavalcante was keeping an eye on Brandao by using an Instagram account under an assumed name.

Then, Cavalcante discovered that Brandao herself posed a serious threat to his freedom: Brandao found out Cavalcante was wanted in Brazil on a murder charge. Brandao made it known she planned to meet with police at 3:00 p.m. on April 19, 2021, to give law enforcement the information on Cavalcante's murder warrant.

Brandao didn't live to alert the police.

Cavalcante didn't wait for Brandao to inform on him. During the afternoon of April 18, 2021, he grabbed a knife and made his way to Brandao's home in Schuylkill Township, Chester County. Brandao and her seven-year-old daughter, Yasmin, and four-year-old son, Yan, were outside their home in the 300 block of Pawlings Road.

Brandao and Cavalcante began arguing. Cavalcante got out of his car and grabbed his former girlfriend by the hair. He threw Brandao to the ground and began stabbing her as her children looked on, horrified. Before Cavalcante concluded his murderous rage, he inflicted thirty-seven stab wounds on Brandao's abdomen, chest, and throat.

Brandao's daughter Yasmin screamed, "Help me! Help me! Help me!" She ran to a neighbor's apartment, saying, "He's going to kill my mommy!" Ryan said the young girl's call to 911 was horrific. According to Ryan, Brandao died looking at her son, Yan. Brandao had her eyes locked on her son, Ryan said. Yan was being held by a neighbor to protect him from Cavalcante.

Brandao died at the scene. Her body was taken to Paoli Hospital, where she was pronounced dead at 4:17 p.m.

Both Ryan and Sassa responded to the murder scene. Ryan recalled it being a gorgeous April afternoon. The scene was not gorgeous. Gathering details was difficult since the victim's family spoke only Portuguese. Helping police to identify Cavalcante as the murder suspect was the victim's young daughter.

Cavalcante was once more on the run. He sought help from friends. Francisco Lima testified at Cavalcante's murder trial that Cavalcante called him and said, "Meet me at the Wawa in Frazer." During the meeting, Cavalcante admitted to stabbing his girlfriend. Lima didn't question Cavalcante as to his motive for the assault or if Brandao was alive or dead.

Lima assisted Cavalcante in cleaning up from the bloody crime. Lima secured water, and the murderer cleaned his hands. Lima gave Cavalcante his hooded sweatshirt to wipe up the blood. Also, Lima consented to be a courier and accepted a bag with thousands of dollars in cash intended for the killer's sister. Cavalcante was paid in cash for his work in construction.

Driving in separate cars, according to testimony, Lima and Cavalcante drove to a storage facility, where they met Michael Scahill. Scahill had a trailer, which he used for his construction business, at the storage facility.

The next stop was Lima's home. The men gathered clean clothes for Cavalcante, retrieved the murderer's fake Puerto Rican driver's license, and stopped to get him some food from a nearby McDonald's. After returning to the storage units, according to testimony, Cavalcante's car was cleaned. Then with the car full of gas and an EZ Pass, Cavalcante drove away from Chester County.

Scahill informed the jury that he had been drinking heavily that day and did not contact police or take any actions to stop Cavalcante from fleeing. Besides, Scahill testified he was "scared."

Cavalcante discarded the murder weapon, according to Ryan, but didn't do a good job of hiding the knife. The knife was quickly recovered.

On the road, Cavalcante's initial destination was Pittsburgh, the same sanctuary he sought after being named in a protection-from-abuse order. This time, his friends told Cavalcante he wasn't welcomed. A domestic altercation was fine with them, but not a murder.

Cavalcante altered his course and headed toward Virginia. Police tracked Cavalcante through his cell phone, and the getaway car was spotted by law enforcement the next day. Back in Chester County, Ryan and Sassa watched the chase and capture from their office in the Chester County Justice Center on West Market Street in West Chester.

Ryan said, "Cavalcante didn't offer any resistance when he was captured. He went as far as falling asleep in the police car as he was transported back to Pennsylvania." The double-homicide suspect—one in Pennsylvania and one in Brazil—was returned to Chester County and the county prison to face murder charges. Breitbart News reported at the time of the arrest that Immigration and Customs Enforcement (ICE) "placed a detainer on Cavalcante, requesting the local jail hold him until they are able to take him into federal custody for arrest and deportation."

For the next two years while awaiting trial, Cavalcante was held in Chester County Prison, the institution that neighbors believed housed only nonviolent criminals. Of course, the US justice system deems a person innocent until proven guilty. Legally, Cavalcante was not a convicted violent offender at that point in the process.

Trials seldom take place in a timely manner, especially murder trials. There are attorneys to engage, court records and police reports to review, and trial strategies to develop. Pretrial motions take time to schedule, argue, and decide. More than two years after Brandao's murder, Cavalcante was brought into Chester County Court of Common Pleas judge Patrick Carmody's courtroom to face a Chester County jury.

The prosecution team of Ryan and assistant district attorneys Zachary Yurick and Monica Szyszkiewicz presented eyewitness testimony of Brandao's daughter and accounts by Schuylkill Township neighbors. Even Cavalcante's accomplices testified for the prosecution. Another important piece of evidence, Cavalcante's statement of responsibility for the murder given to police after his arrest, was introduced.

There was little doubt, if any, that Cavalcante had inflicted those thirty-seven stab wounds.

The testimony, arguments, and Carmody's charge to the jury on the law in the case took about a week. During closing arguments, assistant public defenders Sameer Barkawi and Nellie Verduci, the defense attorneys, acknowledged Cavalcante's guilt. They argued that their client acted in the heat of passion and should be found guilty of a lesser degree of homicide, third-degree murder or voluntary manslaughter.

On August 16, 2023, the jury rejected the defense's argument and found Cavalcante guilty of first-degree murder and possessing an instrument of crime. Deliberations took less than an hour. Cavalcante, now a convicted murderer, was returned to Chester County Prison to await a return trip to Judge Carmody's courtroom to be informed of his punishment.

On August 22, 2023, Cavalcante was back before Carmody for sentencing. The defense attorneys again asked for a break for their client. Barkawi asked Carmody not to impose a consecutive prison term on the possession of an instrument of crime conviction. DA Ryan argued Cavalcante didn't deserve any leniency; Cavalcante's crimes had a devastating impact on Brandao's children.

"The whole family is reeling as a result of this tragedy," Ryan told Carmody before the sentence was imposed. "Not only did he brutally murder Deborah Brandao, but he did it in front of her two children." Ryan called his actions "cold, calculating, and heinous" and noted they had come after he assaulted her on two previous occasions.

Ryan continued, "He wanted her dead. If Miss Brandao went to police, he would have been exposed. He did this to silence her. This was a senseless and heartbreaking tragedy. He butchered her to death."

An account of Cavalcante's criminal past in Brazil was relayed to Judge Carmody by Ryan. Ryan said that Cavalcante had come to the United States illegally in 2017 after having shot and killed a man who owed him money. Although his presence was reported to authorities after his arrest in April 2021, Ryan said she did not believe that an immigration detainer had been filed for his deportation. Normally, she said, immigration cases are not brought until after a defendant has completed their sentence, which in Cavalcante's case will be when he has died.

Judge Carmody provided Cavalcante an opportunity to address Brandao's family. After the judge's prodding, Cavalcante said, "I want to say I am sorry to them."

Cavalcante's brief unemotional and prodded statement was in stark contrast to the impassioned one made by Brandao's sister Sarah. Sarah Brandao recounted how her sister's children are struggling to live after the brutal murder of their mother. Sarah Brandao was raising her niece and nephew, then aged nine and six. She and her husband were in the process of adopting the children. Sarah Brandao's statement was characterized as "moving and heartbreaking" by *Daily Local News* reporter Michael P. Rellahan.

The aunt recounted that her nephew cries for his mother, and her niece sleeps in fear of someone killing her or someone else in the family. "I feel sure that God has given me these children for a purpose," Sarah Brandao said. "I am going to be with them every day. Nothing is going to bring her back. But every day I make the children smile, and make sure our lives will have a new story."

Judge Carmody didn't find Cavalcante to be remorseful. While seated at the defense table and being given a translation by a Portuguese translator, Carmody told the defendant that if he was truly remorseful, he wouldn't have put Brandao's sister and daughter through the anguish of a trial. Carmody added, "For you to cause [the girl] to relive the murder of her mother was a conscious decision by you. It was a selfish decision. You thought of yourself, and you did not think of those children."

In concluding his remarks to the 5-foot-tall defendant, Carmody added in Portuguese, "homem pequeno." Cavalcante's actions were those of a "small man," according to the judge.

Carmody sentenced Cavalcante to a term of life in prison plus an additional two and a half to five years for the weapons charge. Once again, Cavalcante was transported back to Chester County Prison. This time he was a convicted and sentenced murderer awaiting placement in a state correctional institution.

In late August 2023, most of the Pocopson community was oblivious to the fact a dangerous convicted murder was incarcerated behind the nearby prison walls.

CHAPTER 4

CRUCIAL HOURS

Young mother Veronica Horn had an excellent view of Chester County Prison from the bedroom window of her home on West Lafayette Drive. Horn didn't have to travel too far to enter the exercise trail encompassing the prison. The trail was accessed directly across the road from her mailbox.

During the morning of August 31, 2023, Horn went about her normal business. She dropped off her son at a nearby daycare center and returned home with her daughter, who was just several months old. Horn was on maternity leave. She decided to tend to her garden before the heat of the day intensified.

"My doors were unlocked," Horn recalled. "Why would they be locked? We lived in a very safe area. We assumed, as a community, that the prison was doing its job and that we would remain safe at all times. We believed that there was no more of a threat living next to the prison than not living not to prison. Alert systems were in place, we believed."

While Horn gardened, her daughter slept inside the unlocked home, and her son attended daycare. At the same time, convicted murderer Danilo Cavalcante was on the loose, passing fairly close to Horn's home.

Not until 11:00 a.m., more than two hours after Cavalcante gave the slip to prison correctional officers, did Horn become aware that a dangerous felon was roaming her neighborhood. The alert didn't come from a county official; the message came from her son's daycare. Horn was told a prisoner had escaped and the daycare was going on lockdown.

Presently, Horn received visitors, welcomed visitors. "Within thirty minutes of getting the daycare alert, I started to see police in our neighborhood." Those law enforcement officers, along with search dogs, helicopters, and airplanes, would be constant visitors in Horn's neighborhood for days.

The lapse in time from the escape to the warning of nearby residents was frightening to Horn. "A lot could have happened in that time period, and none of it would have been good," Horn said. "Cavalcante could have left the fenced area and been at my door in ninety seconds."

There was an indication that something was amiss at the prison. Horn said she heard the prison's siren going off while working in her garden. "I didn't pay any mind to the warning. The siren goes off every Saturday at noon for a minute. It is a test. The day [Cavalcante] escaped, the siren sounded just like a Saturday test. There was no more level of alertness. The siren didn't continue to sound. If you were in the shower or watching television, you wouldn't have heard the siren."

The overall effectiveness of the prison's siren warning was questioned and criticized by the community. How many citizens can hear and recognize the warning system? Why didn't the siren sound for more than a minute that day?

Chester County has an electronic emergency notification system called ReadyChesCo. The system is designed to send emergency and nonemergency alerts to citizens by phone, text, or email. Emergency alerts, such as the escape of a convicted murderer, aren't automatically delivered. Citizens have to proactively register for the alerts and decide what alerts and government updates to receive. On the day Cavalcante escaped, not every citizen living around the prison had registered. Some didn't know the emergency notification system even existed. After the escaped prisoner was captured, county officials strongly urged citizens to sign up for ReadyChesCo.

Some of the people who were registered for emergency notifications didn't receive updates on Cavalcante's escape. One resident said he received a telephone call alerting him to Cavalcante's capture. He added that he never received a call that Cavalcante had escaped.

For most local residents, news wouldn't reach them until Facebook members and other social media participants started posting accounts during the afternoon hours. Others were first alerted by traditional late-afternoon news reports. For some, many hours passed before friends, family, and relatives from near and far relayed the information of the escaped murderer in their neighborhood. News of the danger that an escaped murderer was in the neighborhood triggered frenzied communications. For almost two weeks, friends and relatives from across the country kept in close contact with those within the police search zones.

Jim Karustis lives close to where Cavalcante was captured. He wrote, "The only semi-interesting thing I can add is that I have a very large family that is scattered throughout the world, and almost every one of them anxiously contacted me during the escapee's 'adventures.' He was 1.5 miles from us, and cousins were nearly constantly messaging me from Argentina, Venezuela, India, you name it."

The first notification given to the Unionville–Chadds Ford School District and its almost four thousand students was somewhat timely but not urgent.

At 10:40 a.m., two hours after the escape, Clif Beaver, principal of the nearby Chadds Ford Elementary School, received a call from Chester County Prison. "All they said was that there was an escapee and no recommendation to go on lockdown," Unionville–Chadds Ford superintendent John Sanville said. "The notification came from somebody from the prison. They wanted to let us 'know we [the prison] are on it.'"

For the moment, the early school year day continued. The high school went on with a scheduled fire drill, meaning that students, faculty, administration, and employees all were outside the building.

Before the escape, the school district and the prison didn't have much of a relationship, according to Sanville. "We provided education to those in the prison still of a school age. That was the extent," Sanville said. "We have a contract with the Chester County Intermediate Unit. Most of the young adults are in the youth detention center. If they graduate, they receive a Unionville High School diploma."

The previous escape of Bolte wasn't reported to the school district. Sanville said, "We didn't know anything about it. There was no notification. I understand that communication isn't at the top of the list when an escape takes place, but communication is necessary, even if a prisoner is quickly captured. A community needs to be informed to stay calm. Absent credible information, you are left with the bloggers and inaccurate information."

Beaver, despite the assurance that the prison authorities were "on it," contacted the district office about the notification. Sanville said that at that point, the elementary school was placed on secure mode. No outside recess was allowed for students, and the doors remained locked.

"The next communication we received was at 12:05 p.m. from an automated call from Chester County Emergency Services," Sanville said. "That one indicated the escapee was a convicted murderer and highly dangerous. This was more than three hours after his escape. He [Cavalcante] could have reached any of our schools in three hours. That call changed everything for us.

"At that point, we had no conversation with anyone in law enforcement. That was a problem for us. The community was upset. We had a fire drill at the high school. The community assumed we knew about the escape [and went forward with the fire drill,] and we did not. The community questioned our actions."

At the time of the escape, Sanville was attending an educational meeting in Harrisburg in connection with his being the past president of the Pennsylvania Superintendents Association. "I was informed of the emergency services notice, and I called George Fiore [executive director of the Chester County Intermediate Unit] and our first responders in East Marlborough. They didn't have a lot of information either."

The early school year day in the Unionville–Chadds Ford School District was no longer routine. "The day was not normal because of the lockdown. All six of our schools were in secure mode. Instruction continued, but no after-school activities took place, and all the students were sent home." The nearby Kennett Square School District also closed its schools. Normalcy in the school districts would be slow in returning.

"At first, there was not a lot of information from law enforcement, the district attorney's office, or the prison," Sanville said. "A lot of people were scared, students and parents, especially if they lived in the developments in the epicenter of the search off Route 52 [near the prison]. The fear escalated because not a lot of information was forthcoming. The situation was made worse by those social media influencers attempting to fill the void. They didn't help reporting misinformation and rumors."

Sanville has knowledge of traditional journalism standards: his father-in-law worked at the *New York Times*. "Journalism has changed," Sanville commented. "The concept of fair, honest, and balanced reporting is long gone. There are no Walter Cronkites working now."

Communications with law enforcement greatly improved when Pennsylvania State Police lieutenant colonel George Bivens arrived on the scene and took charge of the investigation, according to Sanville. Bivens conducted briefings with Sanville and other educational leaders twice a day, once early in the morning, usually around 4:00 a.m., and one late in the afternoon.

The information that Bivens provided contained information on the area being searched. Sanville and the others at the conferences also discussed communications with parents and teachers. "We didn't want to compromise the search," Sanville said. "We talked about information the police were comfortable in sharing. We wanted to be a good partner. The community was scared and stressed. I wanted our communication to our community to keep them calm and reassured. The intention of my communications was to keep everyone calm."

Unionville–Chadds Ford schools were closed on Friday, the day after the escape. Because of the Labor Day weekend, school wasn't scheduled on Monday. The following Tuesday and Wednesday found the schoolrooms silent. One notice posted for parents read "UCFSD will have a Flexible Instructional Day on Tuesday, September 5. All schools and offices will be closed today. Visit our website for more information."

The schools opened a week after the escape, since Bivens made a statement during one of the evening briefings that no reason existed from a safety perspective to keep them closed. "Out of an abundance of caution, we didn't allow after-school activities or sports," Sanville said. "When we reopened the schools, we let students know that this was the safest place to be."

A week after the escape, five schools from the Kennett Consolidated School District—New Garden, Bancroft, Mary D. Lang, Kennett Middle, and Kennett High School—opened and operated on a normal schedule but with an increased police presence on all campuses. The five schools were located outside the state police's latest search perimeter. The only school that remained closed was Greenwood Elementary School, which was within the search zone.

The official message was as follows: "Updated search perimeter that is still within our district borders. Currently, Greenwood Elementary School remains within the search area. Additionally, we are still identifying the various road closures impacting a number of our families. Therefore, tomorrow, September 7, we will be reopening five of our six schools located outside the search perimeter. New Garden, Bancroft, Mary D. Lang, Kennett Middle, and Kennett High School will open and operate on a regular schedule with an increased police presence on all campuses.

"A separate message will be communicated to all Greenwood families with a detailed plan for Greenwood students. For those families electing to keep your children home, the absences will be excused.

"Throughout the evening, we will continue to be in communication with the district attorney's office, Pennsylvania State Police, and local law enforcement to monitor the situation and adjust accordingly based on any new information."

The message to parents from Unionville–Chadds Ford read "Pending information received during the press conference held by the Pennsylvania State Police (PSP), we will be opening Unionville Elementary, Unionville High School, and Patton Middle School campuses beginning today at 4:00 p.m.

"Our intention is to get back to normal as soon as possible and as long as we feel it is safe to do so. Opening the campuses outside of the search zone this afternoon will prepare us to open those schools for students tomorrow. PSP advises that we all be mindful of the numerous road closures that may affect travel. Rapid changes may occur to secure an area so please pay attention and be vigilant.

"As of this letter, Unionville Elementary, Unionville High School, and Patton Middle School will be open tomorrow. If we receive any information that changes this, we will let you know. We plan to review the search zone again tomorrow morning to determine which buildings we can safely open."

Bivens and other members of the state police were fantastic to work with, according to Sanville. "Our school buses were escorted while making school runs, and we were allowed through roadblocks. There was a lot of stress with all the police presence and the roadblocks. We made our students feel safe. From my seat, Bivens did a great job.

"We brought him [Bivens] back to a Unionville football game [after the capture]," Sanville said. "He and one of the search dogs, K-9 Loki, were made honorary captains. Bivens was gracious and he was a star." K-9 Loki had suffered from heat exhaustion while searching for Cavalcante.

First responders were also honored by Unionville students. Second- and third-grade students made and then delivered cards to the Po-Mar-Lin Fire Company, the location for the search's command center for a majority of the hunt. The school district reported, "The [cards were] tokens of appreciation for the brave men and women who have been working tirelessly to keep our community safe over the last two weeks."

Not all the stress and anxiety subsided with Cavalcante's capture. One man reported, months after the murderer was returned to prison, that his grandson was still suffering every time he heard a helicopter—they were omnipresent over the boy's head for days— or heard about a prison or an escape. The young boy displayed systems of posttraumatic stress disorder (PTSD), a mental health condition triggered by a terrifying event, causing flashbacks, nightmares, and severe anxiety.

The boy wasn't the only one reporting anxiety related to the day-after-day saturating search by heavily armed police and constant surveillance by helicopters and planes. Some adults interviewed for his book expressed feeling distressed at times.

When Sanville was asked about Unionville–Chadds Ford students suffering from PTSD, he didn't directly answer. Sanville said, "We have a great team of counselors, social workers, and medical doctors. There was a lot of stress from the situation. Our teachers do a good job. When we reopened the schools, we let students know that this was the safest place to be."

Pocopson Township's government building is within a few minutes' walking distance of the prison. Township officials learned about the escape when Pennsylvania State Police troopers came to ask permission to use the township office for a press conference.

Elaine DiMonte, chair of the Pocopson Township Board of Supervisors, recalls arriving at the township office about 10:40 a.m. to sign some township checks. At the same time, supervisor Raymond McKay was taking part in an emergency services meeting, an ironic happenstance. Neither of the township officials were aware of the morning's escape by Cavalcante when police arrived.

Longwood fire chief A. J. McCarthy was a part of the emergency services meeting. McCarthy was twenty minutes into his presentation on a regional fire department budget when he was interrupted. McCarthy was annoyed by the intrusion. "They said they had a prison escape and wanted the room for the press conference. "I thought they had a prisoner walk away from the work release program. They didn't say a murderer had escaped. I wondered why they couldn't hold the press conference at the prison. They have three buildings."

The reluctance by county and police officials to fully inform the public of the severity of the situation was a mistake, according to McCarthy. "You wouldn't compromise anything by saying a dangerous person was on the loose. People love to use their cell phones. If they saw Cavalcante, they would have called."

DiMonte agreed with McCarthy: "I was told there was an escape," DiMonte said. "I wasn't told the escapee was a murderer. Maybe they didn't want to push the panic button at that time. The notice from ReadyChesCo was received about noon."

DiMonte noted she did hear the prison's one-minute siren warning earlier in the morning. Constituents told her the siren can't be heard from their homes.

Inside the prison, acting warden Holland ordered the prison placed on lockdown and a special count of inmates conducted. At 9:50 a.m., prison officials knew for sure that Cavalcante was no longer residing within the institution. At 10:01 a.m., Chester County's 911 Emergency Center was notified of the escape. At the same time, the prison's escape siren, the one either not heard or ignored by the five thousand township residents and not strong enough to reach the county's half-million population, sounded its forlorn warning.

In Pocopson Township, there was no Paul Revere racing through the township shouting, "Cavalcante is coming. Cavalcante is coming." The township did have Judy Love, an administrator of a township Facebook page.

"On the day the escape took place, I was running the Pocopson [Facebook] group," Love said. "Someone reported they heard sirens and asked if anyone had any information. I put up the question [on Facebook] and suggested maybe a test was taking place. That was about 10:00 or 10:30 a.m.

"Several friends reported they didn't hear anything. I grew up here and lived through other prison breaks. Before, the siren would blast for a good fifteen or twenty minutes before stopping. People knew an escape had taken place. Some local people can hear a train's horn when it passes near the [Brandywine Ace Pet and Farm Store] on Pocopson Road. Maybe the siren was a whistle connected to the train. If the prison would have sounded the siren for more than a minute or two, people would have known it wasn't a train."

Love deemed her community lucky in the hours following the escape, since she believes that Cavalcante wasn't intent on harming anyone as he walked away from the prison and down Wawaset Road. "He could have gone into any house and stolen a car. He could have harmed the homeowner, and no one would have known."

Love reported that the first official notice of the prison break was a little after noon.

One resident who lives on South Wawaset Road, close to the prison, reported hearing the escape siren. The sound was loud and dull, just like the weekly Saturday test. Her husband, who was at home, didn't hear the siren. She didn't want to be identified.

Just before noon, the South Wawaset Road woman received the county's emergency message. The message was that a prisoner escaped, not that the escapee was a convicted murderer. "I closed my garage. I was scared as I heard the helicopters overhead," she said. "I tried to reach out to other people. My next-door neighbor was alerted by her child's school. That was not a good way to warn people."

Another nearby resident, Kathryn Humpfry, lives near the intersection of Routes 52 and 926 on Beversrede Trail, close to both the prison and Longwood Gardens. Her husband and two adult sons work from home. The siren wasn't heard, and no emergency notifications were received at the Humpfrys' household. Humpfry was told of the escape about 2:30 p.m. while teaching in Bel Air, Maryland, about 50 miles away from the prison. "I was about to depart for home when a parent told me."

Dean Ardnell knew something was amiss. Ardnell lived in the Waterglen development and used the exercise path around the prison. Ardnell had a working knowledge of the inside of the prison; he had been incarcerated for alcohol-related charges. "The jail saved my life. I'm a recovering alcoholic," he commented.

Ardnell was planning a trip to the shore for the holiday weekend. About 12:30 p.m., he learned of the escape by a Facebook posting. "By the timing, I knew something was wrong," Ardnell said. "The escape was known by 10:00 a.m. There was no notification. I called my girlfriend, Renee, to make sure our kids weren't at home. Our house was on a direct route. 'He's coming,' I thought. There are one of three ways he could have traveled, and our home is on one of them.

"Not alerting everyone after two hours meant somebody wasn't doing their job. This was botched from the start. They dropped the ball by not notifying the public. They left everyone in extreme danger."

Ardnell's deduction was correct. Waterglen was on Cavalcante's itinerary.

The members of the news media were alerted at 1:09 p.m. by email by the Chester County District Attorney's Office.

As the hours of the first day of Cavalcante's escape passed, not everyone in surrounding areas, of course, knew of the prison break. One person was Laurie Curl. Curl lives in Claymont, Delaware, about 20 miles from the prison. She's not part of the Chester County, Pennsylvania, emergency notification system since she doesn't live in the county or state. Curl said she wasn't paying attention to the local news that day.

That afternoon, Curl received a last-minute work request. A client living in Landenberg, Chester County, decided to go on a cruise, and Curl was needed for immediate pet-sitting duties. Previously, Curl did garden work for the clients but not pet sitting. Curl had never stayed in their home. She agreed to begin work that evening. Curl didn't receive any special instructions from the couple.

Landenberg is about 14 miles from where police were searching for Cavalcante.

During the early evening, Curl learned of the escape. The client's home was large enough for someone to live in one section of the house without being noticed by those in another section. The property also included 4 acres of woodland. This was Cavalcante's desired type of hiding place.

Curl secured the house, lights out and doors locked, and went to bed. She awoke in the unfamiliar house to find lights going on and off in the kitchen area. When she investigated, she found kitchen cabinet doors open. Her immediate thought was that Cavalcante had found his way to the home's expansive basement, taking food from the cabinets. Curl was thinking along the same lines as the escaped prisoner, since Cavalcante did take food from a kitchen and items from a basement after breaking into a home nearer the prison.

A phone call to a friend, Cathy Molique, settled Curl's fear, somewhat, for the evening. "I was in a bookstore in Christiana," Molique recalled. "She [Curl] was scared. She was in this big old house. I told her to call police."

The next day, Curl did as suggested and dialed the Pennsylvania State Police. The responding trooper asked what Curl wanted him to do. "Search the house and grounds," she told the trooper. Curl wanted to feel and be safe. The trooper was skeptical, since law enforcement believed that Cavalcante was contained near Longwood Gardens and was trying to travel north toward Phoenixville and not south toward Landenberg. The requested search was conducted, and the results were negative.

Curl's fearful reaction was typical of so many residents during the next two weeks after a Cavalcante sighting, credible or not, was reported.

Curl discovered the cause of the frightening goings-on in the kitchen that night. Her clients failed to inform her that the lights were motion detectors and would turn on and off with any movement, including their cats. They also failed to mention that the pet cats were proficient in opening kitchen cabinets by pounding on the door with their paws.

By the end of the first day, word was spreading that Cavalcante, convicted of a brutal murder in Chester County and wanted in connection with a second murder in Brazil, was free and desperate to keep his liberty. Cavalcante had little to lose if he killed again. The community had good reason to be fearful.

The prison administration's assurance that they were "on it" was found to be wanting. The escape became a curious global story of intrigue on multiple continents that would last for almost two weeks.

CHAPTER 5

FIRST RESPONSE

The immediate hours after a crime is committed is a crucial time period in any police investigation, including escapes. Any delay in notifying law enforcement provides a criminal an opportunity to escape or destroy evidence of his crime. The sooner law enforcement officers begin their investigation, the better for the public's safety.

A popular television show, *The First 48*, details the first two days of murder investigations across the country. As the show intones, the odds of catching a murderer greatly decrease if the crime isn't solved in the first forty-eight hours.

Cavalcante didn't get a forty-eight-hour head start, but he was free for more than an hour before the prison's 911 call was registered with Chester County's emergency services. Another hour would go by before law enforcement would gather in strength to begin the search for the convicted murderer.

Was Cavalcante still in the vicinity of the prison when the search began? If the escape was carefully planned and the murderer had recruited accomplices with a vehicle, Cavalcante would be long gone from Chester County and possibly on his way to foreign climates. After all, he did flee his native Brazil for the United States after being accused of murder.

Even if Cavalcante was alone without immediate assistance, an hour or two would be plenty of time to trek miles or ensconce himself in the dense underbrush surrounding housing developments, businesses, and cultural attractions surrounding Chester County Prison. He needed some luck in not being spotted.

Upon receiving the prison's 911 call, Chester County's emergency services department contacted county officials, including the county's commissioners, district attorney, and chief county detective. Also, Pennsylvania State Police was notified of the escape. Pocopson Township doesn't have its own police department. The state police patrols the municipality and has the jurisdiction to investigate and prosecute crimes in the township, including the prison.

Not included in the first alert were the surrounding police departments in Birmingham, Kennett, and Kennett Square. All were closer to the prison than the detectives in West Chester and the state police barracks in Avondale and Embreeville. Birmingham police chief Thomas R. Nelling said his notice came about 11:45 a.m., almost two hours after the 911 call. Nelling operates a one-man department, and he wasn't sure how much assistance he could give that day and the upcoming search.

At the Chester County Justice Center, chief county detective Sassa immediately issued an "all-hands order" for his detectives to become involved in the hunt for the murderer. Sassa said he contacted other law enforcement agencies and informed them of Cavalcante's flight to freedom. Sassa was assured that help would be there as soon as possible.

Within two hours, Sassa and district attorney Ryan reported that state police troopers and members of the US Marshals Service were at the prison, the first designated command post for the hunt for the escaped murderer. Later, the headquarters would switch to the bigger Po-Mar-Lin Fire Department in Unionville.

"Hundreds of people were soon working," Sassa said. Sassa noted that the hunt for the escaped murderer would become the biggest case of his career. "I always knew we were going to catch him. I was confident," Sassa said. "I didn't know when or where or the final outcome, but I was confident."

By the time the prison's command post was up and running, Cavalcante had a four-hour head start. The number of possible locations where the murderer had fled was growing. Cavalcante could easily have made his way to the neighboring states of Delaware and Maryland and to major transportation centers, such as Wilmington and Philadelphia. Soon, erroneous reported sightings from the public would place the murderer in many different locations, including Wilmington and West Chester.

The Chester County Prison Board and the county's administrative staff were notified of Cavalcante's escape approximately five minutes after the escape was discovered and reported to acting warden Holland, according to Rebecca Brain, public information officer for the county. From that time, according to Brain, the county's administration was given updates on the search for Cavalcante.

As governmental assets were poured into the search for the missing murderer, the lack of K-9 search dogs immediately dispatched to the scene was noted, especially by those formerly employed by the Chester County Sheriff's Office and the prison.

West Caln police chief Curt Martinez recalls that a call for search K-9s went out the first day of the escape. Dogs from the state police and other agencies in the region responded. Martinez, a sixteen-year police chief, has worked with trained K-9s for twenty-four years. His dog Matrix was ready to track Cavalcante. "I don't go on the initial call," Martinez said. "I did so the next day. I was assigned to a local SWAT team, and we went to an area off Route 952. I did so the next several days."

Former Chester County sheriff Carolyn "Bunny" Welsh was proud of the K-9 unit she assembled for her sheriff's office during her tenure as an elected official. The K-9s numbered eight, and they all were trained trackers, along with a special talent. Some of the dogs were trained to find drugs, and others could detect explosives, accelerants, and dead bodies. By the time Cavalcante escaped, only a few K-9s were at the disposal of Sheriff Fredda Maddox. Maddox succeeded Welsh and is now a judge on the Chester County Court of Common Pleas. Welsh left the sheriff's office in 2001, when Maddox was elected.

"I don't know how long it took them to get the K-9s to the scene," Welsh said. "We could have been there within minutes. My theory is if we had those dogs there, we would have taken him back into custody by the end of the day. We would have had an immediate response with multiple tracking dogs." Holland agreed with Welsh. At a town hall meeting after Cavalcante's capture, Holland was quoted as saying, "If we had dogs, we would have gotten him that day."

The effectiveness of the dogs is tied to the freshness of the scent of the person being tracked.

Welsh said that multiple dogs would have been needed to conduct an effective search. Because of the heat, the dogs would have to be switched out of active service after about ten or fifteen minutes. The search dog would be placed in a vehicle to freshen up, and another K-9 would be substituted, according to Welsh. At least one K-9 needed medical attention during the search. Welsh believes that the K-9 was left working in the sun too long.

Welsh's K-9s were called to the prison a number of times during her tenure. Former warden Ed McFadden, according to Welsh, contacted her if he (McFadden) believed a nasty situation was brewing at the prison. "Inmates would look at the dog, not that the dog was threatening, and just the dog's presence deterred a lot of things," Welsh said.

A depleted K-9 unit wasn't the only missing resource from the sheriff's office. John Freas, a former member of the Chester County Sheriff's Office under Welsh and a former correctional officer, said the sheriff's office once had a fugitive apprehension unit. Those deputies were specially trained in tracking and finding wanted persons. Freas remembers working directly with the US Marshals Service to serve warrants.

A number of issues were cited for the cut in services by the sheriff's office, including money. Elected officials in Chester County didn't heed the English proverb "A penny wise and a pound foolish," often cited by political philosopher Benjamin Franklin. Surely, the cost of the escape, estimated in the $20 million range for taxpayers and businesses, would have kept eight K-9s in kibbles and bits for a number of years.

An open public debate, with heavy political overtones, developed over the lack of K-9s. Maddox, a Democrat, was quoted in an article by the *Delaware Valley Journal* as saying the sheriff's office K-9s were cut in half because of death and injuries to the dogs, a shortage of dog trainers, the departure of her K-9 team supervisor after he was injured, and a lack of funds.

Maddox told the publication that the K-9 unit wasn't totally directly funded by county taxpayers, and private donations were used for vet bills, food, and bulletproof vests for the dogs. After Welsh, a Republican, left office, she was investigated by Chester County and state officials and arrested by the state for the misreporting of donations for the dogs and other administrative actions involving the use of staff at private events. Welsh eventually pleaded no contest to charges. She didn't admit guilt but accepted punishment. Welsh and many others believe that the charges were vigorously pursued by then Democratic attorney general Josh Shapiro, later Pennsylvania governor, because Welsh was an active and visible supporter of Republican president Donald Trump.

When Maddox left the sheriff's office to become a judge in January 2024, she said she didn't expect funding to increase for the K-9 unit. Maddox acknowledged the valuable assistance that K-9s provide to law enforcement. "They have enhanced skills that complement law enforcement personnel's abilities," she said. Indeed, K-9 Yoda of the US Border Patrol was involved in the apprehension of Cavalcante.

Welsh, the former sheriff, believes that Maddox was making excuses in the article, and blames Maddox for the demise of the sheriff's K-9 unit. "The bottom line is the canine program was never supported or encouraged under her leadership," said Welsh. Welsh was quoted in the *Delaware Valley Journal* article as saying, "When I left, we had eight K-9s in service. All were German shepherds except one Belgian Malinois. A ninth dog was a courthouse comfort dog.

"When this Cavalcante character went over the wall, my position is, if we had these dogs engaged before [the trail] was contaminated, because he was on foot, we could have had this guy in a day, even in the sweltering heat. We didn't have the dogs. The unit was decimated. They were down to two [dogs]. Even with six dogs, they could have gotten him."

Besides the K-9 unit being diminished, the number of deputies had been depleted. One report indicated that forty deputies departed the office from the time Maddox became sheriff to the escape of Cavalcante. As 2024 began and a new sheriff, Kevin Dykes, took office, a lack of deputies was a major security concern at the county's justice center. Dykes reported twenty-six vacancies, more openings than in counties adjacent to Chester County. Dykes, Maddox's second in command in the sheriff's department and a former Chester County detective and Pennsylvania state trooper, searched for qualified candidates.

When the justice center employees, on the day before Cavalcante's escape, talked about an impending and inevitable security breach, a major part of their concern was the lack of trained sheriff deputies to guard and transport prisoners and to patrol courtrooms and the justice center entrance. Freas agreed, saying, "There was not enough security for courtrooms. They resorted to probation officers running security. Probation officers have extensive training, but not for courtroom security. In my opinion, a security breach was waiting to happen."

On at least one occasion, the lack of personnel from the sheriff's office accounted for a member of the county's probation office to be stationed inside Judge Carmody's courtroom when Carmody was handling criminal cases.

The month following Cavalcante's capture, President Judge John Hall signed an administrative order setting new guidelines for security and inmate transportation that allowed private security personnel to carry firearms in the courthouse, guard courtrooms, and provide prisoner transport. The Chester County commissioners approved an $880,000 contract with Costa Security Group, of Philadelphia, to provide courthouse security.

One cause for a lack of deputy sheriffs under Maddox's reign was Maddox's requirement that all new deputies had to be certified as municipal police officers. That condition inhibited some otherwise qualified people from applying to Chester County, according to critics.

Whether knowingly or unwittingly, Cavalcante picked an advantageous time to escape from Chester County Prison. Both the county's prison and sheriff's office were understaffed. The once-robust county K-9 unit was decimated. Security issues from a previous prison breakout hadn't been corrected, and a new warden, albeit an acting one, was on his first day on the job.

Security was far from operating at 100 percent on the morning of August 31, 2023. Community members weren't as safe as they believed.

CHAPTER 6

FIRST SIGHTING

Wawaset Road is not a heavily traveled road by motor vehicles, let alone by pedestrians, at any time of the day or night. Even with the scarcity of traffic, most days a lone figure walking south and away from the prison would not be noticed or a cause for alarm.

At about 9:40 a.m. on Thursday, August 31, 2023, a Pocopson resident recalled seeing a man strolling on South Wawaset Road. His route would take him away from the prison and toward housing developments and Pocopson Home and to Route 926. If he continued south, busy Route 1, a byway to Philadelphia, Wilmington, and even Baltimore, was within a twenty-minute walk. Turning west on Route 926, a walker would find the back entrance to Longwood Gardens. The resident saw the lone walker about an hour after Cavalcante crab-walked the prison wall.

The man fit Cavalcante's description. The stranger was small in stature, according to the resident. Officials at the day's press conference described the escaped murderer as being slight and 5 feet tall and weighing about 120 pounds, with shaggy black, curly hair and brown eyes. To the resident, the man's outfit didn't scream out that he was a prisoner. Officials reported that Cavalcante was last seen wearing a white T-shirt, gray shorts, and white sneakers.

Cavalcante was not sporting a bright-orange jumpsuit with the letters CCP stenciled on the back or front, as the public expected. The Chester County government administration was severely criticized by the public for allowing prisoners to dress without some designation that the person was an inmate. A change in the dress code oversight was one of a number of changes at Chester County Prison brought about by Cavalcante's escape.

The reported sighting of a man on foot was a clear indication that Cavalcante didn't have immediate access to transportation. Police focused the initial searches on the area surrounding the prison.

An alert from the Chester County District Attorney's Office concerning the lurking murderer was posted on the Longwood Fire Company's Facebook page about noon that day.

POCOPSON TOWNSHIP, PA—August 31, 2023—Officials of Chester County Prison report that at approximately 8:50 a.m., a prison inmate, Danelo Cavalcante, escaped from Chester County Prison. A search of the prison and surrounding area is currently being conducted.

The subject is described as a Brazilian male who speaks Portuguese and Spanish, light skinned, 34-year-old, 5-foot, 120 lbs., with shaggy black curly hair and brown eyes. Subject was wearing a white t-shirt, gray shorts, and white sneakers.

Notification of the escape has been communicated to all residents within a six-mile radius of the prison. Chester County Detectives and the Pennsylvania State Police are conducting a thorough county-wide search, and prison officials are conducting an internal investigation.

Anyone with any information on the whereabouts of Danelo Cavalcante is asked to call 9-1-1 immediately.

Chester County district attorney Deb Ryan said, "Danelo Cavalcante is considered an extremely dangerous man. We are asking for the public's help in locating him. He was last seen walking on Wawaset Road in Pocopson Township around 9:40 a.m. wearing a white t-shirt, gray shorts, and white sneakers. The defendant is also wanted for a 2017 murder in Brazil. Law enforcement is doing everything now to locate him. If you see this individual do not approach him. Call 911 immediately."

Further information will be provided in a press conference held by Chester County district attorney Deb Ryan at 2:00 p.m., at Pocopson Township Building.

The Longwood social media posting contained an obvious omission. The fact that Cavalcante was a convicted murderer wasn't noted, only that he was suspected of one in Brazil. Another part of the posting was wildly inaccurate. As many members of the community soon attested, by noon not everyone, by a long shot, knew of the escape. "Notification of the escape has been communicated to all residents within a six-mile radius of the prison" wasn't accurate.

Ryan was on her way to the prison by 11:30 a.m., as one news account reported. The district attorney once again had Cavalcante intruding in her daily professional life. Earlier in the month, Ryan and Cavalcante spent days together in the courtroom of Chester County Court of Common Pleas judge Patrick Carmody for Cavalcante's trial and sentencing. Except for posttrial appeals, Cavalcante should have receded from the district attorney's daily work schedule. Because of the escape, once again, Cavalcante would dominate the district attorney's professional life for the coming weeks.

Ryan knew Cavalcante was dangerous and deadly. Details elicited during Cavalcante's murder trial made it clear the Brazilian was a cold-blooded killer. During the first-day press conference, Ryan implored, "If you see him, do not approach him. We're asking you please to contact 911. He is considered extremely dangerous."

The admonition to stay clear of Cavalcante would be ignored by many civilians in the coming days. The lure of a reward, $20,000 at one point, was enough for many people to take up weapons and enter dense Chester County thickets to find the elusive diminutive Brazilian. The bounty seekers either forgot or ignored the warning that Cavalcante was desperate, wanted his freedom at all costs, and had killed at least one person, maybe two, and wouldn't hesitate to murder again.

With Ryan at the press conference was acting warden Holland. Holland's first day on the job would be one he will never forget or wish to repeat.

Holland told the assembled reporters that "a single point of failure" was to blame for the prison break. A correctional officer guarding the exercise yard was using his unauthorized cell phone at the time, reporters were told. The escape, Holland indicated, was through a triangular open space above the exercise yard. Yard 6 was the designation used during the press conference.

During the press conference, Holland failed to mention many other factors contributing to the escape. No mention was made of prison officials knowing that Cavalcante had escape plans weeks before his trial. No mention was made that the triangular open space was used in a prior prison escape and was never properly secured. The public hadn't been told of the previous escape. The fact that the prison, the sheriff's office, and the K-9 corps all were severely understaffed wasn't part of the briefing.

Even though the "single point of failure" excuse would be used more than once by county officials, the county government failed in multiple ways to properly secure Chester County Prison against a breakout. "There were multiple points of failure," Fire Chief McCarthy commented.

An initial reward of $10,000 was offered for information leading to Cavalcante's capture, the public was informed.

Pennsylvania State Police troopers, members of the US Marshals Service's fugitive task force, and Chester County detectives immediately began their pursuit of Cavalcante. The original search area was a 6-mile radius of Chester County Prison. Members of law enforcement had multiple resources at their disposal, including helicopters and drones. Later, search planes with infrared-heat-identifying equipment were deployed against the lone diminutive Brazilian.

Arrangements were made at the Brandywine Airport in West Goshen to be able to access their fuel truck 24-7 even when the airport was closed, a police officer reported. He added that members of the elite Pennsylvania State Police's Bureau of Special Operations conducted patrols with night-vision drones. "With the high tree canopies and thick woods, drones flying high over top of the trees often could not see what was on the ground underneath. If a possible sighting was called out over the radio, the drones quickly were re-deployed to that area," the police officer wrote. A bogus tip reported to police had Cavalcante hiding and sleeping in trees.

The seekers would need all the modern devices to find, locate, and arrest Cavalcante. Professional law enforcement officials with experience in locating criminals worked diligently and long hours to find the elusive murderer.

One of the areas searched the day of the escape was Baily's Dairy, near the prison. Meredith Parsons reported that police walked the perimeter with flashlights. "They thought Cavalcante might have traveled through our property," Parsons said. "Police never returned to search the farm. During the following days, we knew he was in the area, but we didn't believe he was on our property."

Parsons, as did many of her neighbors, criticized police and government for not fully disclosing information about Cavalcante. She commented, "I wish we would have known earlier that he was so dangerous. Kids were at school bus stops when he escaped. We all believed the prison was full of DUI and child support criminals."

Cavalcante was roaming in the area first identified as the search area. Later, the murderer told law enforcement that initially he didn't move a great distance. Robert Clark, supervisory deputy of the US Marshals Philadelphia office, said Cavalcante had "hunkered down in a very, very secluded" area of Chester County, heavy with woods and undergrowth.

In an interview with *Newsweek*, Clark related, "He didn't move for the first couple [of] days. He survived on a watermelon that he found at a farm. He drank stream water. He was hiding his fecal matter under leaves and foliage so that law enforcement couldn't track him. He was a desperate man."

Later, Cavalcante admitted that officers came within 5 or 6 feet of his hiding places and almost stepped on him three times during the search. Despite being so close to the murderer, the law enforcement members couldn't detect Cavalcante. Clark commented, "That just proves to you how thick the vegetation and the foliage was."

A number of obstacles made the search difficult. First, the search area was extremely large. The heat was oppressive, since most search days the temperature soared past 90 degrees. The underbrush was thick and full of prickers and stinging insects, as some of the searchers attested. When they were carrying full tactical gear, more than 50 pounds of extra weight was added to members of the search team. One of the searchers said he "had plenty of scarring on his arms. The bushes were hard to walk through. It took a lot of time."

As the search dragged on for days, onlookers, residents, and thousands of people across the world following the hunt on social media expressed surprise that the lone escapee wasn't in custody. They were baffled by the lack of success in finding Cavalcante. What was taking so long? Why didn't the police utilize the knowledge of locals to guide them? More than one suggested that police should link arms, walk into the fields, and find Cavalcante. All the friendly suggestions, police knew, had flaws.

First, a large army would have been needed to link arms to cover the 6-mile search area. Second, searching the rugged underbrush wasn't as easy as it seemed. "The Pennsylvania woods are relentless at times," said US marshal Eckman. Eckman described an experience he had during one of the searches after a reputed sighting of Cavalcante. "It was so dark we were using flashlights and our gun lights to light our way. I went in 20 or 30 feet in the undergrowth, and it was so thick, I bent down. I could only see a small animal trail system. I had nowhere to go. I backed out."

McCarthy commented, "People were terrified. Some sheltered on the second floor of their homes. The residents of Waterglen were scared. The public assumed Cavalcante would be quickly captured. People didn't understand the terrain. I told them Cavalcante survived the jungles in Brazil; Chester County would be a walk in the park for him. The police were relentless. They chased the guy the whole time."

One of the investigators was stung thirty-two times by hornets, and another agent had an allergic reaction to pollen, Clark reported. Eckman and other seekers testified to fighting the nasty prickers of the thickets. Sassa reported that some of the searchers couldn't see 5 feet in front of them. Longwood Fire Company provided EMS services. McCarthy reported that besides the bee stings, one police officer was hit by a car.

For most residents and visitors, Chester County's rolling hillsides are full of picturesque horse and dairy farms, preserved fields, and sprawling developments with plenty of open space. Off the traveled paths, unnoticed, is the summer terrain, consisting of thick and almost impenetrable underbrush and dense woods.

Cavalcante wasn't the first person to use the terrain of Pocopson and surrounding municipalities to mask movements. He wasn't even the first escaped murderer to do so. Cavalcante, unknowingly, had history on his side.

Don McKay's family has lived in Pocopson Township for generations. Many members of the McKay clan have farmed the rich fields of the area. McKay family members have taken leadership roles in the township. Don's father, Raymond, was a township supervisor at the time of the escape.

Don McKay knows the township like the back of his hand. During a ninety-minute personal tour of Pocopson on January 7, 2024, Don pointed out locations where his family members lived over the years. McKay also pinpointed locations where Cavalcante was reportedly sighted during the search. During the pursuit, one of McKay's relatives needed his hay harvested. A search for a killer couldn't delay the farmwork; the hay needed to be cut. The harvesting took place as heavily armed law enforcement members patrolled the edge of his fields.

The exhaustive Cavalcante search took place in an area where history was made. As the private tour developed, McKay recited a number of other Pocopson historical facts.

Pocopson Township was part of the Underground Railroad system in the years before the Civil War. Escaped slaves made their way north and some spent a night or two in Pocopson. After spending some time in the township and surrounding Chester County communities, the freedom seekers continued on their trek, eluding the slave catchers. The concealing terrain of the township made the runaway slaves difficult to find.

On the township government property, across from the prison, sits a home known as Barnard Station. Eusebius Barnard was born in 1802 and was a Quaker. A founding member of the Longwood Meetinghouse, he supported human rights. Putting their own lives at risk, Barnard; his wife, Sarah; and their children offered shelter to those seeking freedom. Barnard died in 1865, after Lincoln's emancipation decree and the Civil War had concluded.

The Barnard stone farmhouse was built in the early 1800s and has received recognition as a historic structure from the National Park Service and the Commonwealth of Pennsylvania.

As escaped slaves used the natural cover of trees and thickets to make their way north on Wawaset Road to freedom, Cavalcante was utilizing the same cover as he reversed the direction of the slaves, heading south on the road to his freedom. Later, Cavalcante switched directions and went north.

Pocopson Township was in the thick of another historical event on September 11, 1777, during the American Revolution. Early in the morning the vaunted British army, under the command of General William Howe, was camped at nearby Kennett Square. Howe was on a quest to capture the American capital at Philadelphia. In his way was the army of General George Washington, behind the Brandywine River.

The year before at Long Island, New York, Howe split his army, outflanked Washington, and almost captured the rebel army. Howe decided to use the same tactic on September 11. He ordered a little less than half of his army to drive the American light infantry in front of the British army back to the Brandywine. Howe and General George Cornwallis led the remaining portion of the British army on a flanking maneuver, covering more than 14 miles, to reach the rear of Washington's army.

For Howe's plan to work, Washington must not be alerted to the splitting of the British army. Of course, Washington well-remembered the thrashing at Long Island and vowed not to allow Howe to fool him again. Washington sent out scouts that morning but didn't receive definitive information on the location of the British army.

Howe's clandestine route took him through portions of Pocopson Township, the same area where freedom-seeking slaves and convicted murderer Cavalcante sought cover. A morning fog helped shroud the movements of the British forces. If a farmer happened to see the British army, the farmer was detained, so the farmer couldn't alert Washington. As the British forces made their way through one densely forested section, an officer wrote in his journal that the location would be a perfect place for an ambush. Concealed American forces wouldn't have been detected. However, no rebel Americans were along the route, and the British continued their march to the rear of Washington's army, almost unmolested.

Howe's plan almost worked to perfection. Several British officers wrote that if they had several more hours of daylight, they could have forced Washington's forces to surrender. Daylight faded, and brave and fearless individual actions by Washington's troops, including future American hero the Marquis Lafayette, saved the American army to fight another day. Young Frenchman Lafayette was wounded on Birmingham Hill as he tried to rally Washington's troops against Howe's forces.

The Pocopson terrain played an integral part in Howe's plan, as the territory later did as part of the slaves' escape route and as camouflage for Cavalcante.

When Cavalcante escaped, a good chance existed that the murderer had never heard of Norman Johnston and his murderous brothers Bruce and David. While aware of Bolte's short-lived freedom after escaping from Chester County Prison, Cavalcante's knowledge was limited, if he had any, of escaped prisoner Norman Johnston's sojourn in 1999 in some of the same terrain Cavalcante covered in 2023.

The Johnston brothers went to nearby Unionville High School. Many of their gang members were also from the Kennett Square–Unionville area. Another convicted murderer, Ancel Hamm, went to Unionville High School. The gang members, led by Bruce A. Johnston Sr., became proficient in the criminality of theft. They were known to steal anything not tied down. They stole from Longwood Gardens and from the Brandywine Museum of Art. They stole tractors from farmers in Pocopson Township and many other regions of the country. They stole truckloads of tractors from dealerships. In fact, when the Johnston brothers were plying their trade, more John Deere tractors were stolen in the tristate area of Pennsylvania, Delaware, and Maryland than in the rest of the country combined.

Heavy construction equipment and Corvettes were two additional items favored by the Johnston brothers. The gang members were rightfully feared by most of the community. Many just tried to stay out of their path. The gang had several rules, including that no cooperation with police was ever allowed. If a gang member was arrested by police, the gangster would quietly serve his sentence. "If you can't do the time, don't do the crime" was a favorite gang saying. The Johnston brothers would do anything, including murder, to stay out of prison.

The Johnston Gang members became brazen and violent. When Kennett Square policemen attempted to bring Hamm, the Johnstons' safe expert, to justice, Hamm murdered officers William Davis and Richard Posey. He was the only person charged and convicted of the crime. Bruce Johnston told his brother-in-law Roy Myers that he (Bruce) and brother David Johnston were involved in the murders. When criminal Gary Crouch decided to inform on the gang, Bruce Johnston and another gang member, paid hit man Leslie Dale, shot and killed Crouch on a dirt road in a secluded section of the county just north of Pocopson Township. Crouch's body was buried in the secluded area and not found until Dale cooperated with police and led them to Crouch's grave.

After state, county, and local law enforcement and the FBI started to close in on the Johnston brothers, the brothers murdered witnesses, including members of their own gang. Bruce Johnston Sr. murdered his stepson and ordered the death of his son, Bruce A. Johnston Jr. Norman and David Johnston, the intended victim's uncles, ambushed Johnston Jr. and his fifteen-year-old girlfriend Robin Miller in August 1978. Johnston Jr. was shot multiple times and survived. Miller, pregnant at the time, died.

Johnston Sr. was convicted of taking part in six murders. His brothers David and Norman were found guilty of first-degree murder in four killings. All were sentenced to multiple life imprisonment terms in state prisons in 1980. They were gone but not forgotten. Those in Pocopson and throughout Chester County believed they were through with the Johnstons. Not so.

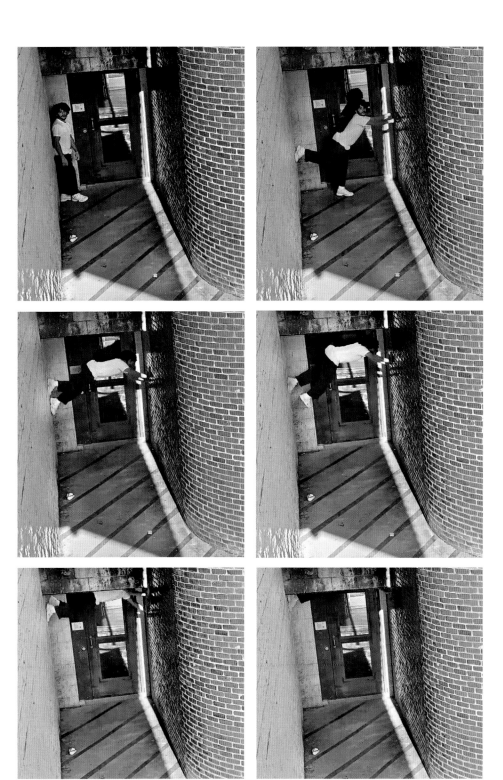

Convicted murderer Danilo Cavalcante is shown crab-walking up prison walls as he escaped Chester County Prison on August 31, 2023.

WANTED

REWARD: Up to $20,000
WANTED FOR: ESCAPE

Danelo Souza Cavalcante

WANTED SINCE:
8/31/2023

CAUTION — VIOLENT HISTORY

Case Outline:

IN:
Chester County, PA

Combined reward is now up to $20,000

FOR:
Escape (Serving life sentence for homicide)

Danelo Cavalcante is wanted by the Chester County Detectives, Pennsylvania State Police, and the United States Marshals Service (USMS) for escaping from the Chester County Prison on 08/31/2023.

Cavalcante is also wanted for homicide in Brazil. He is a Brazilian national fluent in Portuguese and Spanish.

DOB: **07/03/1989**   Race: **Latino**

Sex: **Male**   Hair: **Black**

Height: **5'00"**   Eyes: **Brown**

Weight: **120**

Anyone with information on his whereabouts should call 911, PA State Police command post at 1-877-926-8332 or anonymously contact the PA Crime Stoppers at 1-800-4PA-TIPS (8477) or https://www.p3tips.com/tipform.aspx?ID=107.

Report any information on his whereabouts to 911 or the PA State Police immediately

This fugitive is considered extremely dangerous

A Pennsylvania State Police wanted poster offers a reward of $20,000 for information on escaped murderer Danilo Cavalcante. "Danelo" was one of the first names used to identify Cavalcante.

Escaped murderer Danilo Cavalcante was captured on a Ring doorbell camera in the Phoenixville, Pennsylvania, area several days before his capture.

Escaped murderer Danilo Cavalcante changed his clothing and appearance by shaving during his escape. He is seen on a Ring doorbell camera photo.

Daily press conferences were held while murderer Danilo Cavalcante was on the loose. Seated at the table (from left) are District Attorney Deb Ryan, Pennsylvania State Police lieutenant George Bivens, and Chester County chief detective David Sassa.

An aerial image is shown at the time murderer Danilo Cavalcante is surrounded and captured.

The photograph was taken moments after law enforcement members took convicted murderer Danilo Cavalcante into custody.

Captured murderer Danilo Cavalcante is led in handcuffs to an awaiting car to be taken to Pennsylvania State Police barracks at Avondale, Pennsylvania.

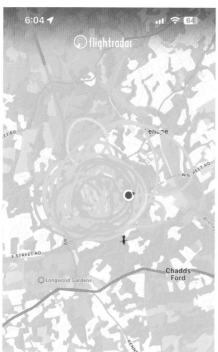

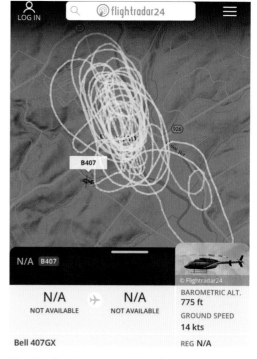

Helicopters were omnipresent for almost two weeks in the skies over Pocopson Township, Chester County. The flight tracker app gave residents an idea of the paths of the helicopters. Longwood Gardens, where murderer Danilo Cavalcante hid, is noted on the map.

Months after the capture of murderer Danilo Cavalcante, residents of the area suffered emotional trauma when hearing helicopters. Helicopters were constantly in the skies for almost two weeks, and residents followed the paths on computers.

An area of the prison is shown where murderer Danilo Cavalcante made his escape after crab-walking up prison walls.

The area of Chester County Prison where murderer Danilo Cavalcante escaped is in the process of being secured by Chester County officials.

Barbed wire is part of the deterrent used by Chester County officials to keep inmates inside the prison.

Murderer Danilo Cavalcante used the same escape route utilized by another prisoner weeks before Cavalcante crab-walked up and out of Chester County Prison.

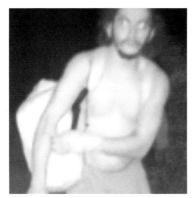

U.S. MARSHALS
WANTED
REWARD: Up to $5,000

WANTED FOR:

Escape

Danelo Souza Cavalcante

Aliases:

WANTED SINCE:
8/31/2023

IN:
Chester County, PA

FOR:
Escape (Serving life sentence for homicide)

DOB: 07/03/1989   Race: Hispanic
Sex: **Male**   Hair: **Black**
Height: **5'00"**   Eyes: **Brown**
Weight: **120**
Scars/Tattoos:

CAUTION-VIOLENT HISTORY

Case Outline:

Combined reward is $10,000 ($5,000 from USMS and $5,000 from Chester County)
Danelo Souza Cavalcante is wanted by Chester County Detectives, Pennsylvania State Police and the United States Marshals Service (USMS) for escaping from the Chester County Prison on 8/31/2023. Cavalcante is also wanted for homicide in Brazil. He is a Brazilian national fluent in Portuguese and Spanish.
Anyone with information on Cavalcante's current location should call 911 or contact the U.S. Marshals Service at
1-877-WANTED2 or online at usmarshals.gov/tips.

NOTICE TO LAW ENFORCEMENT: Before arrest, verify warrant through the National Crime Information Center (NCIC). If subject is arrested or whereabouts known, contact the nearest U.S. Marshals Service office, American Embassy/Consulate, or call the U.S. Marshals Service Communications Center at 1-800-336-0102.

USMS Tips Code   **Report any information to the U.S. Marshals:**   USMS Tips

📞 1-877-WANTED2 (926-8332)   🌐 usmarshals.gov/tips

In 1999, Norman Johnston was housed in one of the most secure state prisons at Huntingdon, about a two-hour drive from Pittsburgh. The prison had been Norman's home since 1987. Norman was not a model inmate. He was placed in the restrictive unit of the prison after breaking regulations. His punishment was being confined in his cell for twenty-three hours a day. The extra hour was used for exercise and a shower.

On Sunday evening, August 1, 1999, Johnston was seen in his cell preparing to retire. By morning, Norman was no longer in his cell or the prison. Like Cavalcante, Johnston had been planning an escape for some time. Unlike Cavalcante, Johnston had active assistance. A correctional officer and a nurse admitted smuggling packages to Johnston. Both employees were suspended and dismissed. The prison employees claimed they believed the packages contained personal items, such as gum, and not the tools Johnston needed to escape.

Once Johnston's absence was noted, Huntingdon prison officials initiated a search and used helicopters. Helicopters would be omnipresent during the Cavalcante hunt. A portion of Johnston's cell window had been removed and a section of the prison's fence was cut. Also, a Land Rover car was stolen from the prison grounds.

Two days after Johnston's escape, Pennsylvania State Police put together a document detailing information about the Johnston Gang, including associates, crimes they committed, and photographs of the Johnston brothers. The document was distributed to law enforcement.

Even though he was about 130 miles from Chester County, Johnston decided to return home, an area where police would surely be searching for him. Did he return for revenge? Did he return to clear his name? Did he want to roam a familiar area? Was he seeking financial assistance from friends and relatives? All were motives attributed to Johnston. The murderer needed assistance from friends, relatives, and cohorts, even though his presence in Chester County increased his chances of being captured.

Johnston being on the loose caused those who testified against him and helped send him to prison to be on edge for weeks. State police troopers guarded key members of the prosecution team.

A state police release announced that Johnston, who stood 6 feet, 1 inch tall and weighed 180 pounds, was to be considered armed and dangerous. "He's proven he has no respect for human life, and he's going to be very desperate," one prosecutor said.

The public warnings about Johnston applied equally to Cavalcante. A desperate murderer was on the loose.

A manhunt in the Pocopson area commenced. Residents reported locking their doors, and those endangered kept loaded weapons at the ready. Johnston's escape was featured on the television show *America's Most Wanted*, and a $40,000 reward was offered for information to aid in Johnston's capture.

Twice law enforcement believed they had Johnston in their grasp. On August 6, 1999, two park rangers sighted Johnston in West Nottingham. One grabbed Johnston's shirt. The fugitive broke free, ran into woods, and eventually stole a car to escape. A woman was convinced she saw Johnston in Fair Hill, Maryland, just over the Pennsylvania line. The man was gone by the time the woman called 911 and police arrived.

On August 10, Norman Johnston's forty-ninth birthday, a task force searching for Johnston expanded to forty persons—less than a tenth of law enforcement personnel dispatched to search for Cavalcante. The public supplied hundreds of tips and reported sightings. For almost three weeks, all the public's help went for naught.

Both convicted murderers were operating with handicaps. Cavalcante didn't have assistance, and he didn't know the terrain. Johnston had some help, and he knew the area but he was technically deficient. Being locked in a prison cell for two decades meant that life's improvements bypassed him. He couldn't operate modern gas pumps. Cell phones and ATM cards weren't available when he went into prison. He could steal only older-model cars. The workings of new cars baffled Johnston, a master of car thefts when he roamed Chester County two decades earlier.

Finally, in the early-morning hours of Friday, August 20, 1999, Norman Johnston was taken into custody by ten Pennsylvania State Police troopers. He was cornered in a housing development that had been a farm when Johnston was incarcerated. The back of the development was fenced. Johnston had nowhere to run. After almost three weeks on the loose, Johnston was returned to prison.

Johnston, the same as Cavalcante, had little to say about his time on the run. Pennsylvania State Police captain Henry Oleyniczak reported at the time Johnston that indicated he had a "daily struggle to survive with police dogs constantly on his trail." Oleyniczak added, "The best we can tell from our encounters, he was living in the woods a lot." Johnston did tell police he hid out by day and went to convenience stores for food at night only, listening to the radio newscasts and reading newspapers to keep one step ahead. Johnston declined to talk to reporters when he was taken into custody.

Johnston faced trial on the escape charge. A Jefferson County, Pennsylvania, jury convicted Johnston after fifteen minutes of deliberations. The trial took three hours. Johnston claimed that the escape was the result of being locked in isolation for the better part of seven years. Johnston was ordered to spend another forty-two months in prison after he completed his four consecutive life imprisonment sentences. In other words, Johnston will never be free; that is, unless he escapes again. His brothers Bruce and David died while serving their sentences.

Johnston later said his big mistake was not fleeing the area. He told the police he spent days hiding and nights looking for food. Without knowing, Cavalcante copied the same pattern during his escape.

CHAPTER 7

THE SEEKERS

The immediate response was impressive. Manpower, needed to search for the escaped murderer, arrived quickly at Chester County Prison, the initial command post for the hunt. Chester County chief detective Sassa spearheaded the marshaling of forces. Sassa's past positive experiences working with the agencies fostered cooperation.

The first alerts outside Chester County government agencies went to the Pennsylvania State Police and the US Marshals Service. The marshals, along with the state police, are key members of the Eastern Pennsylvania Violent Crime Fugitive Task Force. The task force was the first of its kind in the United States, originating in 1981. Members of the task force were kept busy in 2023 as Cavalcante and other absconding criminals kept the task force busy. One newspaper dubbed 2023 the year of the prison escapee.

Robert Clark, supervisory deputy of the US Marshals Service for the Eastern District of Pennsylvania, was the first marshal to arrive at the scene of the escape. "Sassa reached out to me the first day and asked for assistance. I responded to the prison. I was attempting to get a feel for what was taking place," Clark said. "Dave was in charge. The county detectives were handling everything and did so for the first few days. The county detectives did the best they could with their resources."

Clark was an experienced seeker. He began chasing fugitives for the Marshal Service in 2009, fourteen years before Cavalcante escaped. While majoring in English at East Stroudsburg University, Clark became interested in law enforcement. A career decision loomed when Clark was forced to decide about his future education. By continuing in school, Clark could obtain the degrees necessary to teach. By taking an offered job in law enforcement, Clark could begin his favored career path. His mother told Clark to stay in school. Clark took the job at the offered Monroe County Correctional Facility. After a year and a half, Clark advanced to a position in Philadelphia where he worked with the Marshals Service. He then joined the marshals.

Regarding those first few days of the search for Cavalcante, Clark said, "We were all hoping that someone would uncover the right rock and he would be there. The problem was the amount of ground to be covered was huge."

Fire Chief McCarthy said the assumption of a quick capture caused initial issues. After learning of the escape at the Pocopson Township building, McCarthy reported that police didn't contact the fire company until midnight on Thursday evening. Police believed they had Cavalcante pinned down in the woods and requested an ambulance to stand by. The fire company had only two ambulances available to cover the region for the public's use, but McCarthy assigned one for the search.

The next day the ambulance was still committed, and McCarthy knew that Cavalcante had eluded the search party. That Friday morning, McCarthy was getting a haircut when he received an urgent call to get to the prison as soon as possible. McCarthy did so and stayed at the command post at the prison through the Labor Day weekend.

Because all were hoping for a quick capture, no planning for logistical support was made. How were the searchers going to be fed? How were they going to be kept hydrated in the extreme heat? How were medical services to be provided?

"In the beginning, the command was unorganized a little bit and challenging," McCarthy said. Because of the Labor Day holiday weekend, Pennsylvania State Police resources were limited. When a decision was made, the state police representative left the meeting and called his commanding officer to gain approval. McCarthy said an "intervention" was held on Saturday, and steps were taken to formulate a clear command structure.

Longwood Fire Company began supplying food, water, and medical assistance and continued to do so for the remainder of the search in the Longwood area. "We used our supplies," McCarthy said. "Then we contacted Good Fellowship [of West Chester] and used the supplies they had on hand."

As for food, members of the community and area businesses contributed. Land Hope Farms donated breakfast sandwiches, Wawa made sandwiches, and Walmart donated food and water. Arrangements were made for supplies to be picked up as needed. Delaware County FOP brought its food trailer. "I drove an ambulance and filled it with food; that will give you an idea of the supplies needed," McCarthy said. When items were required, the community was alerted and residents supplied the material, according to McCarthy.

The logistics were staggering. Longwood members inventoried supplies and set a schedule. Between noon and 2:00 p.m. and then from 6:00 p.m. to 7:00 p.m., food and water were available for shift changes. Food and snacks were handy twenty-four hours a day. "We were using thirty to forty cases of water a day and fifteen to twenty cases of Gatorade. Wawa hoagies were packaged a hundred to a box, and we were using six or seven boxes per shift change." Manfredi Cold Storage of Toughkenamon donated a unit to keep supplies fresh.

One of Clark's first calls on Thursday went to Marshal Steve Eckman. Eckman, a tactics and firearms instructor, was conducting a training course in Atlantic City when Clark dialed his number. Clark briefed Eckman on the Cavalcante escape. Eckman asked if he should forgo the remaining part of the training course and immediately report to Chester County Prison. Clark told Eckman he would be expected at the prison the first thing the next day.

Clark, Eckman, and hundreds of other law enforcement members reported to Chester County every day for almost two weeks. To many of the officers, the county became a home away from home. Their shifts were long, since many worked overtime. For some, the endless hours conducting the intense search seemed like they were working around the clock. Clark said that he spent one night in his truck, sleeping for a few hours. He didn't want to be too far from the command post in case a break in the search took place.

Organizing and directing a large force from multiple agencies is an immense task. Representatives taking part were from local departments, county departments, Pennsylvania agencies, and federal branches. They all had their own hierarchy and modes of doing business.

The Marshal Service isn't a large agency, as Eckman commented. "The state police can bring a lot of bodies. When we [the Marshals Service] arrived, we contributed our resources. The state police and county detectives from the district attorney's office were running the operation. We were all trying to work together. We didn't know each other."

Vying for leadership and the responsibility for planning the search operation could have been an issue. District Attorney Ryan said that after three days, she knew additional assistance was needed. She reported talking to some of her peers around the state, and all told her she needed "Bivens." That is, she needed Pennsylvania State Police lieutenant colonel George Bivens to spearhead the team.

At the time, Bivens, sixty-one years old, was the state police's deputy commissioner of operations. The Johnstown, Pennsylvania, native joined the force in 1985 and took part in a number of high-profile investigations during his career.

The FBI quickly joined the team. Assistant special agent in charge James Milligan said that FBI agent Dan Tantino of the Newtown Square office alerted him to Cavalcante's escape. The FBI had been involved in the prosecution of Cavalcante's murder case, providing translation services. "We have a good relationship with the [Chester County] DA's office," Milligan said.

When Bivens took charge of the manhunt, Milligan called to offer assistance. "We dealt with Bivens on the Frein manhunt several years earlier," Milligan said. "I also met him on several other occasions. I called him, and he said give me ten minutes. He [Bivens] then returned my call and said our [FBI] help was needed. We offered tactical assistance."

Clark and the marshals worked with Bivens, along with the FBI, on the capture of killer Eric Frein. In 2014, Frein murdered Corporal Bryon K. Dickson II, a thirty-eight-year old Pennsylvania State Police trooper, and seriously wounded Trooper Alex Douglass.

The search for Frein lasted forty-eight days before the murderer was captured at an abandoned airport.

"We were familiar with Bivens from the Frein investigation," Clark said. "Our [US Marshals] SOG [special-operations group] found Frein in a hangar some years ago. It was best decision to bring him [Bivens] in for the Cavalcante search. He had just completed another manhunt in western Pennsylvania."

In December 2023, Ryan gave Bivens the Chester County District Attorney's Office "Law Enforcement Officer of the Year" award for leading a two-week manhunt resulting in the capture of escaped killer Cavalcante. Ryan commended Bivens for leading an "unforgettable manhunt" that left Chester County at a standstill for two weeks while hundreds of first responders searched for his whereabouts.

"Our community was front and center on a national and international stage as we faced one of the greatest challenges law enforcement has seen in this county," Ryan said. "Bivens brought a long-decorated past into his efforts during the manhunt that resulted in Cavalcante's capture."

Once Bivens arrived, a different command structure for the Cavalcante hunt was put in place, according to Eckman, who was the lead investigator for the Marshal Service. Clark was the supervising officer for the marshals. Bivens was in overall charge.

Early difficulties needed to be solved, including communications among law enforcement agencies. The agencies had different systems. The Pennsylvania State Police had an encrypted radio system. At points in the search, the system was decrypted to allow other agencies to hear messages and receive up-to-date news. The decrypted radio frequency also meant that astute members of the public could also hear the broadcasts. A fear was that the information would make its way to Cavalcante.

Hostage negotiators were placed on standby in case Cavalcante broke into a home and took family members hostage. Medical assistance was also placed at the ready in case law enforcement, civilians, or Cavalcante needed care.

Dr. Bert Schiffer, an EMS medical director, was involved in the medical support for the search teams. "Medical assets were available for many days," Schiffer said. "It was very hot and miserable. Most of the operators were frustrated they couldn't find Cavalcante, but they went out every day. We had a fairly robust rehab for officers, cover [from the sun], and [fluids for] hydration. No member of law enforcement was transported to a hospital as a result of the search.

"Every day varied, depending on the situation. The command and control structure leadership changed a number of times during the operation. First it was local, then state and federal. The structure changed radically with the state police. There was a change in the flow of information; it was more circular. The information was shared in real time and coordinated. A lot of agencies were involved, and they all were cooperative, especially late in the search. It was excellent teamwork."

The command post was moved from the prison to the Po-Mar-Lin firehouse in Unionville. For days, the small Unionville community, west of the prison, was jammed with traffic from the police, news reporters, and the public. Staging areas for quick-response teams were designated. At times, the Karco gas station, a Longwood Gardens parking lot, and Owen J. Roberts High School were used to gather law enforcement assets for the search.

McCarthy was consulted on possible locations for the new command post. His own Longwood Fire Company was too cramped and couldn't offer the needed space. Po-Mar-Lin was possible, and McCarthy contacted Po-Mar-Lin. At first the space was to be used for several trucks and some of the team of searchers. Then, a decision was made to move the whole command post to Unionville.

A key component of the command restructuring was the gathering of a team of ranking officials from each agency. Information received and processed was passed to the team and then disseminated to the field operatives. That command structure allowed all the varied agencies to efficiently gather, disseminate, and utilize intelligence during the Cavalcante investigation.

Sassa added, "A tactical and investigative plan was designed, and the details were adjusted as needed."

The instituted command structure, according to Eckman, was modeled after a recent similar search in western Pennsylvania. That search was for Michael Burham, who crab-walked out of a Warren County jail on July 6, 2023. A week later, Burnham was back in custody. Burham was camping when police were alerted. With the help of a bloodhound, troopers took Burham into custody. "That's been our strategy all along, to push him hard, have him make a mistake," Bivens told reporters at the time of Burham's capture. "He finally did."

As for the Cavalcante hunt, Eckman said, "The county and state police did the technical and command and we did what we do; we catch fugitives." Before the search was concluded, about two-thirds of the staff from the US Marshals Eastern District Office was involved. Radios, camera systems, and other materials were supplied by the federal agency during the hunt.

The FBI's contribution included SWAT team participation from various FBI offices. In the Frein investigation, SWAT teams were brought in from across the country. Since the manhunt for Cavalcante was in a smaller footprint, local teams, including from Newark, New Jersey, and Philadelphia, took part, according to Milligan. Often, the FBI teams covered swing shifts as part of the twenty-four-hour surveillance, Milligan said. One outcome, an important one, should be highlighted from the search for Cavalcante, according to Eckman. "All these agencies came together and worked as one giant team," Eckman said. "I've never seen it before. I could ask any of the organizations for assistance, and I would receive it. When we were asked, we provided everything we could. The state police is a phenomenal organization with a ton of resources and skills. The same goes for the county detectives, the border guys, and [the US Department of] Homeland Security. They are all skilled and highly respected."

Milligan added, "The partnerships were formed over the years and were already strong. You walk away appreciating the professionalism [of all the agencies]. The marshals, Immigration, Pennsylvania State Police, DEA, State Game Lands, and the border agents all gave exceptional efforts. We were proud to be part of the team. Such teamwork pays dividends in other investigations." Not long after Cavalcante was captured, the FBI worked with Clark and the US marshals on the murder of a Philadelphia law enforcement officer. "Rob [Clark] is a great partner," Milligan said.

Besides experience, Bivens brought a no-nonsense presence and a resolute conviction that Cavalcante would be captured. As the days passed and the public became restless, Bivens remained steadfast. The murderer would be seized.

During the search, the team received hundreds of reports from the public. The command post vetted each sighting and each report. A decision was then made as to the action to be taken on the sighting, or not taken.

"We were concentrating on where [Cavalcante] was going," Clark said. "How could we get ahead of him? Establishing proof of life was a challenge. A lot of tips were called in. They were trying to be helpful. I believed what we saw on the trail cameras. Time and again, he was caught on the trail cameras. The trail cams were so important. We were relieved when we had the first trail cam video of Cavalcante. The images verified he was still in the area."

The cameras were so vital that every available camera under control of the law enforcement agencies was contributed to the cause of finding Cavalcante, and additional cameras were purchased.

According to Eckman, after social media postings, everyone in the specified area believed they saw Cavalcante. "They wanted to be helpful. Definitely, social media was a double-edged sword. We ended up sending resources to areas where the reported sightings might not have been credible."

For the most part, troopers from the Pennsylvania State Police were on the scene first to check on a reported sighting of Cavalcante. Eckman said the command structure cut down, but didn't eliminate, two agencies acting on the same tip. "Sometimes the troopers were there first to investigate a tip, and sometimes we would arrive later. Sometimes we were the first ones to respond. The command coordination eliminated much of the repetitive work. We were all on the same page."

There is a difference in the way the state police investigators and the Eastern Pennsylvania Violent Crime Fugitive Task Force members operate. "The troopers are great investigators. They just work a different way," Eckman said. "They verify reports and information and take action. We need information now, not tomorrow. If we waited for confirmation, the fugitive we were seeking would be long gone."

A report during the first weekend of the investigation needed an immediate response. A search plane from the Pennsylvania Attorney General's Office reported that someone was spotted walking in the area near the prison. A team of seekers was organized and launched. The investigators heard noises and speeded up the pursuit. As the team closed in on the suspected location of Cavalcante, the source of the commotion was determined. A family was hosting a Labor Day weekend party, including a full barbecue.

Cavalcante was not a guest at the barbecue. Reported sightings and rumors continued to flow during Friday. Most of the reports were false. Later in the investigation, officers joked that the best way to capture Cavalcante was to have everyone barbecue. The smell would drive the hungry murderer insane.

DA Ryan informed the public on Friday, September 1, 2023, that, so far, information indicated Cavalcante was still in the area of the prison. Ryan speculated that Cavalcante might be attempting to move south and return to his native Brazil. Also, Ryan reported that no one appeared to be assisting the murderer.

One of the more outlandish rumors reported on social media was that Cavalcante had slipped the police perimeter and made his way to Wilmington, Delaware. In the port city, Cavalcante stole a boat and was on the open sea, heading back to Brazil. Such incredulous reports highlighted the problems with social media.

The outlandish Wilmington rumor was cited by West Chester *Daily Local News* reporter Michael P. Rellahan as a reason his newspaper chain didn't chase after every social media rumor. The chain didn't have the resources, since Rellahan was the principal reporter covering Chester County. "I couldn't cover the story full time as I was still responsible for stories in the courthouse on the courts and commissioners," Rellahan said. Rellahan didn't receive direct orders on how to cover the case for his readers. He coordinated coverage with editors sitting in Reading, Berks County.

Rellahan covered the daily press conferences and made a sojourn to the country prison the weekend after the escape. The reporter wanted to talk to acting warden Holland but was told Holland wasn't taking questions. Despite the lack of resources, Rellahan commented, "We were keeping up with the larger news organizations."

Social media, according to Rellahan, had lots of speculation but not much real news. Rellahan recounted one rumor having Cavalcante immediately fleeing to West Chester and St. Agnes Church on Gay Street. At the church, the fugitive received a hot meal and change of clothes. Rellahan didn't believe that Cavalcante even knew his way to West Chester, let alone where St. Agnes was located, even though it was less than a block away from the Chester County Justice Center, where the murderer was tried and sentenced.

West Caln police chief Martinez said that both social media and traditional media caused issues. "I received a call from a colleague saying he was shown in the background of a Fox News report. That means everyone watching knew our [search] location and movements," Martinez said. "The YouTubers bugged me at times. They stayed near the police and reported what they heard, and about half of what they reported was inaccurate."

Judy Love said one of the social media streamers was encouraging civilians to be armed and to go into the fields searching for Cavalcante. The streamer was intimating that it was prudent to do so, according to Love.

One local journalist with national experience, Rich Heiland, opined in the *Unionville Times*,

> By far, most citizens exercised caution, and many called in tips. But this episode should have taught us that citizens also can become a part of the problem. For instance, television news featured several people who were basically the same kinds of people who slow down to look at a car wreck. One man talked at length, as if he were some kind of expert, about how he drove to the most active part of the search area. He said he just wanted to see it, talked about conversations he had with officers. Seriously? Not good. As a print journalist I would have walked away from someone like that and not given them a second of fame. But TV is a different animal.
>
> Another fellow featured in the media drove up from Maryland. He brought his drone with him and would drive around the search area to fly it. He told interviewers he had a gun so he wasn't in danger. Police took a dim view of his activity.
>
> It may be too much to expect that every citizen in a search zone will act responsibly. It may be too much to hope for that every citizen will realize this is real life, not a TV show or spectator sport, and stay the hell out of the way of the professionals.

As the total number of tips and rumors concerning Cavalcante's whereabouts surpassed the century mark, nearby West Chester University decided to cancel classes to help protect its 15,000 students. The school's campus is located about 6 miles from the prison. Cavalcante could have walked to the university within several hours of his escape. Access to all university buildings was limited to those possessing a West Chester University identification card or key.

Residents in Pocopson, West Chester, and beyond were heeding calls to lock doors and be extra careful. Simsun Greco, who lived in the gated East Goshen community of Hershey's Mill, made sure her doors were locked and secure, and advised her neighbors to do the same. Hershey's Mill is more than 15 miles from the prison.

Search teams scrambled into action early Friday afternoon. An attempted burglary was reported in the 1100 block of Ballintree Lane in Pocopson Township. The home was just off Wawaset Road, between the prison and the Karco gas station at the intersection of Routes 52 and 926. An initial investigation couldn't confirm that Cavalcante was involved in the attempt to break into the home.

West Caln police chief Martinez was involved in a number of the early searches. He said he worked with local SWAT teams in the area of Route 952. "At one point a neighbor reported Cavalcante running in the woods, and we searched nearby homes to make sure he hadn't entered them, Martinez said.

While on patrol, a neighbor and a Pennsylvania state trooper reported seeing Cavalcante, according to Martinez. He also was involved in a search after a neighbor reported finding a screen door ripped from a back door. The homeowners weren't home at the time.

Michele Lynch and her husband, Darryl Fink, live in Tullamore, a thirty-three-carriage-home development in Pocopson Township off Route 926 and close to the prison. Even though alerted to Cavalcante's escape, the couple felt safe among their neighbors. "I didn't know Cavalcante's history. I never heard of him. I always thought it [Chester County Prison] was a white-collar-crime prison," Lynch commented. "I was surprised he was a murderer. We had notification to secure in place. Our whole neighborhood knew we were to secure in place."

On Friday afternoon, Lynch was reading on her deck when she said she heard a "crunch, crunch, and then nothing and then crunch, crunch." Because of the summer foliage, she did not have a clear view of the walking path in the woods behind her home. Lynch then saw a lower part of a body. She called for her husband to come to the deck. He didn't see anything, but then they both heard two additional "crunch" steps. They called police.

Police arrived within five minutes of the call and interviewed the couple. Police also secured the video from the home's surveillance camera. Lynch described the walking path and noted that the trail ended at a cul-de-sac in the development, not far from their home. The officers walked the trail and the perimeter but didn't venture far into the woods. K-9s didn't respond with the police to the call. The police were busy that afternoon. Lynch reported hearing the officers receiving "two or three calls" during the time they were at her home.

Lynch said that the person she saw in the back of her home, believed to be Cavalcante, had plenty of time to disappear into the dense woods before the search commenced. She wanted to make sure one of her neighbors wasn't the person spotted, so Lynch contacted them to make sure no one was walking their dogs at the time of the sighting. No neighbor was on the trail.

A Lynch family celebration was scheduled for Labor Day weekend. Lynch and her husband hesitated about holding the gathering before going forward with the celebration. "My mother-in-law was flying into town for the first time in eight years. We had a wedding, and both of our children were here Saturday night, Sunday, and Monday," Lynch said. "We didn't know if we should have the party. Helicopters were circling for days. When they were still flying in the morning, we knew they didn't capture him the night before.

"We weren't too concerned. [Cavalcante was] not going to break into a community where so many eyes would be on him. We had people come over, and they stood on our deck but did not venture beyond to the trail. Our ninety-two-year-old uncle drove from Philadelphia and had to go through roadblocks. My daughter joked she came to the suburbs for all of the crime. At our hot tub, we had a butcher knife and a dog.

"My husband walked our dog, not too far, in the field. At one point, both helicopters came down towards him. He waved at helicopters and pointed to the dog. One circled higher than the other."

The moving roadblocks and detours made traveling to Delaware for a legal appointment difficult for the Lynch family. "Every day the roadblocks were in a different place, and we had to turn around and try different routes. We left early to go anywhere. We were fine with the precautions taking place. We offered coffee and water, and they were polite and nice."

Lynch's mother-in-law had planned to visit Longwood Gardens for the first time. She never saw the gardens.

During late Friday evening, police had solid evidence that Cavalcante was loose in the Pocopson neighborhoods and seeking supplies—food, clothing, and weapons—from area homes. No longer would there be a doubt that Cavalcante was a menace to the citizens of the community.

One resident, Ryan Drummond, encountered Cavalcante and experienced an "acute moment of terror," as he told CNN's Michael Smerconish. Drummond and his family live in the 1600 block of Waterglen Drive. Drummond's home is close to Ballintree Lane and about a half mile, he said, from the prison "as the crow flies."

Drummond testified at Cavalcante's preliminary hearing on escape, theft, and breaking-and-entering charges on February 2, 2024, before magisterial district judge Matthew Seavey in New Garden Township. The following is his account from his sworn testimony and comments made to Pennsylvania State Police troopers and reporters.

On the evening of Friday, September 1, 2023, Drummond checked all the doors and windows in his home before his family turned in for the night at about 9:30 p.m. His family included his wife, Meaghan, and three children, aged ten, seven, and two. All the entrances were secured except for one door. There was a problem with the lock. The old French door was closed but not bolted. Earlier in the day, as he sat at his deck overlooking some of the community's dense, cloaking undergrowth, his eldest daughter reported some trepidation over the unsecured door. Drummond assured his daughter that Cavalcante was far from their home and wouldn't menace them.

The family slept in second-floor bedrooms until Drummond heard a noise about 11:40 p.m. Drummond investigated. He made his way, silently, to a second-floor railing. There he could view the French door. The door was ajar. Drummond alerted his wife to the noise and the open door and asked her to call 911. The father of three then checked on the safety of his children. State police reported receiving the call at 11:42 p.m.

Standing at the doorway to the bedroom, Drummond grabbed a picture frame to use as a defensive weapon. Meaghan Drummond joined her husband, and from their position on the balcony they could see their "dim" kitchen light going on and off. There was no doubt an unwanted intruder was in the home. Drummond testified that the hallway light to the kitchen went on and off three or four times. Drummond flicked the hallway light as a warning to Cavalcante that he knew the murderer was in the house. Drummond believes Cavalcante flicked the kitchen lights as a warning to stay upstairs.

"I saw a male coming out of the kitchen," Drummond testified. "He had on a white shirt, and he then walked out of the opened door. He had a skinny build." State police trooper Brian McCabe reported that Drummond told him the intruder was wearing a "baggy white T-shirt, a backwards white baseball cap, [and] dark pants or shorts, and he had dark hair." Drummond told McCabe that Cavalcante ran into the woods and appeared to have either a bulky white backpack or a pillow case.

No words were spoken between Drummond and the intruder. Drummond said he was never on the same floor of the house with Cavalcante. About thirty seconds elapsed from the time Drummond saw the light from the kitchen to the time the man walked out of the door. When he first saw Cavalcante, Drummond told reporters, his "stomach dropped."

Police searched the family's backyard with flashlights. They were too late; Cavalcante had disappeared within the dense foliage.

Under the watchful eye of McCabe, a search of the kitchen area and the first floor of the Drummond home took place. Discovered missing from the kitchen were some produce, apples, peaches, and snap peas, recently purchased from a farmers' market, and Drummond's white baseball cap. McCabe reported they went to the basement of the house, and Drummond reported no items were missing.

Drummond made sure his firearm was secure. The gun was untouched.

The close encounter with Cavalcante frightened his family. Drummond said he took additional security precautions. He made sure each door was locked, installed a video doorbell, and learned more about his firearm. For four days, a SWAT team was in his yard. They were patrolling as he set up a soccer goal for his children.

A few days after the break-in, Drummond told reporters, "The last few days have been surreal. It's tough. We're all jumpy, and I could see this has taken a psychological toll on my kids. If they're in the room by themselves, they're calling for us." As each night passed and the manhunt intensified in his neighborhood, Drummond reported that the fear stayed with him and his family.

Most nights, Drummond reported hearing noises or seeing a light flash in the kitchen. "The paranoia is there," he was quoted as saying. Even after the murderer was captured, Drummond reported standing on his upstairs balcony, with a bat in hand, listening for any movement. He didn't sleep well, and for months he had daily conversations with friends and neighbors about his night of terror. Helicopters evoke an emotional response every time he hears them.

Not until September 26, 2023, did Drummond discover that other items had been taken from the basement of his home. Troopers McCabe and John Pisker showed Ryan and Meaghan Drummond some items found near Cavalcante after he was captured. The items included a Gillette razor, a new shirt, his daughter's purple sleeping bag, a backpack for a camera, and a steak knife. All were taken from the Drummond's basement. A police report valued the items stolen at $252.

Cavalcante was loose in the neighborhood, armed with the knife. Video from a residential surveillance camera recorded the murderer in the 1800 block of Lenape Road at 1:43 a.m. on Saturday, just two hours after Drummond had spotted Cavalcante in his home. The video depicted Cavalcante walking through a wooded area, emerging from behind a small tree and wearing a backpack, the one taken from Drummond's home.

CHAPTER 8

FEAR AND PRECAUTIONS

At first, the escape of Danilo Cavalcante didn't cause great concern on the property of the Kendal-Crosslands Communities. Since the retirement complex was several miles away from the prison, residents and staff weren't deemed to be in any immediate danger. Certainly, Cavalcante was not in the market for a move to a retirement home.

Kendal-Crosslands is home to nine hundred residents, six hundred staff work in the four villages, and a daycare center operates on the grounds. The retirement villages began in the 1970s and were made possible by a grant from the Philadelphia Yearly Meeting of the Religious Society of Friends. It is a Quaker community, holding fast to the Quaker values of community, stewardship, empowerment, and purpose.

The break-in of the Drummond family home on Waterglen Drive changed everything on the Kendal-Crosslands property.

Kendal-Crosslands borders the Waterglen development. From the Drummond home, the escapee could easily walk to Kendal-Crosslands in a few minutes. Such a route would have been advantageous for Cavalcante. The retirement community offered the escaped murderer many prime hiding and resting places.

The property contains 500 acres of woods and meadows, and a meandering nature trail. At the time of the escape, not all the housing units were occupied, since some residents were on vacation and visiting families during the Labor Day holiday. So, Cavalcante could have easily secured himself inside a vacant home.

An emergency meeting of Kendal-Crosslands management was held Saturday at noon. Lisa Marsilio, chief executive officer; Seth Beaver, vice president of community operations; and Michele Berardi, senior director of communications and public relations described the measures taken to keep everyone safe and to calm fears. "People were afraid," Marsilio said.

Both residents and staff needed reassurance as Kendal-Crosslands took on the appearance of ground zero for the search for days. Law enforcement personnel were constantly on the grounds. The retirement center always had a good relationship with law enforcement, but never had the property seen so many black SUV vehicles with heavily armed officers on the property.

"To see those vehicles rushing along our narrow roads for days was a sight," Berardi recalled.

Daily searches were made of the property and the buildings, according to Beaver. Maps of the development were supplied to police to aid in the searches. Also, video from property cameras was provided for police review. When needed, management provided food, water, and bathroom facilities to law enforcement during the hunt.

Police reciprocated with information. Kendal-Crosslands staff utilized the twice-daily updates on the progress to find Cavalcante to plan the day for residents.

Keeping tabs on the location of the residents at all times was essential. Besides some being on vacation, many left the property for dinner and other activities during the day and evening. As much as possible, the property was shut down at 4:00 p.m. Special programs were postponed. Even reaching some areas of the property was difficult since roads were closed in the area, including Route 926, which split the property into two sections. The hiking trail was closed to all for the duration of the search.

Meals were delivered to residents so they wouldn't have to travel in the evening to the dining hall. "We had some practice," Berardi said. "We did so during the COVID epidemic." Beaver said the Kendal-Crosslands staff provided valuable assistance during the dangerous period, with many of them working extra shifts. Housekeeping support continued to be offered to residents.

Before making a final decision on an issue that might affect the search for Cavalcante and the safety of the residents, management contacted police to receive approval. One such issue involved residents tending to their gardens.

"It was hot," Beaver said. "The residents were worried about their gardens. So, we carved out a slot from 8:00 a.m. until 10:00 a.m. so they could tend to their gardens. The police were alerted when we were there. Residents and staff appreciated our [management] concern for their safety," Beaver said.

Staff members weren't passive. Some participated in the searches. Detached buildings, such as one administration building left vacant overnight, were searched before staff members were allowed to enter each day. One of the meadows was sprayed just in case Cavalcante was hiding in the field.

Police stationed at Kendal-Crosslands were kind and courteous to the residents and answered questions. All cars coming and going from the property were checked by police. No matter what time of the day or night, law enforcement was available for questions from management.

There were many reminders that a search was being conducted. Berardi recalls the helicopters. "They were everywhere," she said. Marsilio remembers hearing the voice of

Cavalcante's mother being broadcast from one of the helicopters. The mother was imploring her son to surrender.

For many throughout the whole search area, the constant sight of the helicopters and the sound of the whirls of the helicopters' blades were symbols of the search and initiated a feeling of fear. Long after the search was concluded, the sound of helicopters triggered trepidation.

"There was a lot of craziness out here," Berardi said. Part of Berardi's job was to quell the rumors and provide accurate information. Another part of her job was keeping reporters and social media, especially the "YouTubers," off the property.

"We didn't want to alert Cavalcante that Kendal-Crosslands was a good destination for him," Berardi said. When outsiders attempted to gain access to the property, Berardi made it clear to all that the property was private, not public.

All the efforts taken to keep the residents and staff as calm as possible were successful. One resident of the Crosslands community, William Gallaher, said he and his neighbors were advised to keep off the trails, keep lights on in the house, and keep doors locked. No extraordinary protection was suggested. Gallagher said he didn't believe the murderer would traverse to his development.

"We were grateful Cavalcante didn't come near here," Beaver said.

While Cavalcante didn't physically set foot on the property, his escape caused a major disruption in the lives of residents and staff and instilled fear.

Across the region, individual residents restricted visits from family members and friends. Firearms were part of the safety precautions taken by community members. More than one resident recalled walking their dogs while armed.

One wrote on the Pocopson Facebook page, "Helicopters haven't stopped. They were flying at 2:00 a.m. and all night. I could hear them either close to my house or in the distance. So, do I risk going out to mow and get my dog out?"

Flight tracker became a favorite application of those in the search area. Overhead flights could be watched.

Attorney George Asimos and his family live about 2 miles from the prison, near Parkersville Road. Their home was central to the search for several days. The family heard the noise of constant overflights of the helicopters and airplanes. There were days when the road in front of their home was closed. Asimos recalled state troopers suggesting he take a different route to work. The troopers didn't offer suggestions on an alternative direction, since they were from another part of the state, not from the two Chester County barracks. Those troopers traveled hours to reach Chester County and begin their search shifts.

The day before the escape, Asimos and his daughter were preparing to go canoeing in the Adirondack Mountains. They started on their Labor Day outing, but their holiday vacation was prematurely concluded. "We were following the escape," Asimos said. "A high school buddy of mine, I've known him for forty years, is in law enforcement. He came to our house that first night to make sure everything was secure. I was uncomfortable having my wife, sons, and ninety-year-old father at the house. So, we came home early."

Asimos and his family relentlessly followed the progress of the search. Piecing together the news was not easy. Fox 29 television news and a social media blogger streaming the search were sources of the family's information, as were the alerts from Chester County government. The live blog feeds offered a "ringside seat," according to Asimos. For a time, the ring was outside his living-room window.

Some details were supplied by the mainstream media and Chester County government, according to Asimos, but not enough for the up-to-the-minute developments the family desired. "We also had the daily updates from Bivens. We watched religiously. That was very helpful. They were transparent with us."

Bivens, Clark, and other lead investigators indicated that one of their goals was to be transparent. "My perception," Asimos said, "was the investigators understood the community's fear and inconvenience." As the days passed, there was an appearance that law enforcement was "not on the ball," but Asimos disagreed with that perception. "They were," he commented. "I'm not a critic of the state police. They were amazing to us. They were courteous and responsive."

The days of the search changed the lives of the Asimos family. "We had to enforce complete vigilance," Asimos said. "I told my wife to let me know when she was leaving work to come home. I told her if someone on the road tries to stop you as you are driving, don't stop. I told her I didn't care what she did, don't stop. If you run him over, you'll get a medal. I was sure he would get out of the way. I told her to speed up and get out of the way." Asimos gave the same advice to his seventeen-year-old son.

When Asimos family members arrived in the driveway, they were instructed not to exit their vehicle until an armed Asimos gave them an escort into the home. "That was a moment of danger," Asimos said. "I was armed. I had a gun in my pocket at night. This situation made a case for the Second Amendment. I'd be a wreck for the rest of my life if I killed anyone." Asimos's main goal was protecting his family.

Veronica Horn, who lives next to the prison, recalled how her neighbors adjusted to a new lifestyle. She said, "This was not fun. My experience was not significantly worse than others. I am an empath. I felt scared for everyone in the community as the hunt continued and perimeter changed. We became obsessed with true crime on YouTube. They aren't journalists; they are true-crime enthusiasts. It was hard to determine what was true. We weren't getting what we wanted from law enforcement and media. The reports were old.

"It became an obsession that you be as safe as you can. We were checking on people. Facebook was all-consuming. I think some in the neighborhood were convinced he [Cavalcante] was in our area. Later, police didn't patrol as often, as they believed he had moved. We still had the aviation patrols.

"It was scary. We're not gun owners. People were making do with what made them comfortable. Some neighbors purchased handguns and made sure they were armed when they went to their cars. It was interesting how everybody merged into the lifestyle. For some, they continued with their runs and walking their dogs. It was no big deal. Having a newborn baby, my emotions were heightened. We brought out a machete and we kept our car doors locked. My husband came to the car with me. We slept with knives."

Law enforcement, Horn, Asimos, and others realized that the only way Cavalcante was going to elude the manhunt was for him to steal a vehicle.

"He was a very, very bad guy," Asimos said. "I came to the conclusion he was going to steal a car. That was his only way out. I couldn't understand why he was not long gone. If he couldn't steal a car with keys, then he would get one while people were near the car. He could kill someone. He had nothing to lose. If he got away, he could dump the car and get on a train, and they'd never find him. Our biggest fear was getting in and out of the car and going down the street."

Being fearful is alien to the Pocopson community, or at least it was before Cavalcante's escape. "This isn't a common feeling in our area," Asimos said. "It was difficult to get my family to lock our doors. We are so comfortable. The same goes for most of Chester County. We are pretty safe where we live. It was a big change to have to think about security. That isn't true for many parts of the world and in our country. The safety concern was a realization that we are in the same boat as a lot of people. We hear of shootings every day in the streets of Philadelphia. There are more reports of carjacking incidents. We were put in the middle of this fear."

Asimos wasn't alone in commenting for the book that crime can happen anyplace, even in Chester County. With three decades of law enforcement experience, Kennett Township resident Brian Sprowal can attest to the fact Chester County is not immune to lawbreaking.

Sprowal, a member of the Philadelphia Police Department, was working with the Delaware Valley Intelligence Center at the time Cavalcante escaped. The intelligence center is described as a collaborative and proactive agency dedicated to forecasting, preventing, and responding to all threats, hazards, and major events in the region. "When an incident with criminal and terrorist implications occurs overseas or on US soil, it is our utmost responsibility to ensure that our public[-] and private[-]sector partners have accurate and timely information in an effort to protect our communities and critical infrastructure," the organization's website stated.

Sprowal and his family, including twin nine-year-old sons, settled in Kennett pre-COVID. "I moved the family to Chester County for the quiet and peacefulness," Sprowal said. "All was so until the prison break. Nothing like this had happened in Chester County for years. It is a quiet community, even more so since COVID."

The community offered many places for Cavalcante to hide, including cornfields and creeks, according to Sprowal. "Wow, this is for real," Sprowal said. The realization came when his sons' school was closed and roads in his neighborhood were blocked by the extreme police activity. Sprowal had issues traveling to work, West Chester, and even the Amish Market in Westtown.

As the manhunt continued for days, anxiety in the community built. No longer were garage doors left open. The freedom, liberty, and safety that neighbors felt by neighbors evaporated, according to Sprowal. "So, what do you do? What do your family and neighbors do?" Sprowal commented. Neighbors used Sprowal as a resource. "It was exciting for me to drive in the area and look at the command post. I was playing two parts, a professional law enforcement officer and a community member. Neighbors constantly asked me what was taking place."

One question involved carjacking. The concern was real among police and neighbors. "When asked, I said if confronted, a car is replaceable. Let the individual go."

The fear overtaking Chester County is common in Philadelphia, where Sprowal worked and lived for years. "Gun violence takes place on a daily basis," he said. "It brought tears to your eyes. Life in the city and the suburbs is different. Here, there is a lot of distance between homes. You have to be prepared. Are you protected? Conversations were taking place for the first time about quality of life."

Some of the fear was caused by the misinformation being spread on social media. "I talked with a friend in Florida, and she followed the reports on Cavalcante. She did a deeper dive and discovered [that] what was being reported was impossible to have taken place. People were jumping on the bandwagon, increasing chaos. People were on edge. Helicopters were everywhere. You could see the lights from different aircraft involved. The technology of what we saw at night was amazing."

For Sprowal, he said he concentrated on information that was vetted. "I saw many platforms that were putting out rumors. They were trying to join the hunt. The YouTubers and tweets were competing. You want vetted information." Constable Carozzo agreed, saying, "They didn't know what they were talking about. I stayed away from them."

With all the national and international reporting of the story, Sprowal said friends and family contacted him to see if he was safe. "Calls were fine, but I didn't invite any of them to visit," he commented. The no-visit rule lasted two weeks, a little too long in Sprowal's estimation.

"I believe in the system," Sprowal said. "We all became critical of those who had the responsibility to ensure safety we expect. Not to be critical, but if you had the leadership skills, this never would have happened. We all were happy when the apprehension was made with a peaceful resolution."

Sprowal had several comments on the conduct of some community members, including some friends from the city. The friends asked Sprowal, "What's the reward? We'll get them!" Sprowal didn't think it was such a great idea.

Some of those bounty hunters were seen by residents of Traditions at Longwood, a community described as having "300 single-family homes, two clubhouses, a pool, two tennis courts, four pickleball courts, two community gardens, and other amenities for 55[-]plus active adults."

One of the residents, retired colonel Willard C. Conley of the United States Army, gathered members of the community to discuss the havoc caused by Cavalcante. Taking part along with Conley were Ed Wyatt, Celeste Scozzafava, Gene Rogers, Tom Detweiler, Tony Musacchio, and Kathy Conley.

Cavalcante was unknown to the community before this escape. Because of the proximity, Traditions at Longwood members were aware of the prison, but the institution didn't enter their daily thoughts. "We live in a neighborhood where we didn't always lock doors, especially during the day. We didn't do so when we went for a walk. That has changed. We no longer do so," one member commented. Another said, "Never locked my door before. Now I do. As soon as I come in, I lock my doors."

The community was alerted to the escape by various means, including cell phone calls from worried friends and family members. Others received notices from the county's electronic notification system. None heard the prison siren. They are too distant for the sound to carry.

The distance from the prison to the development was an easy walk for Cavalcante, if he wished to do so. Because the community is bordered by woods, Traditions at Longwood was a possible hiding place for the escaped murderer. Many believed he would quickly be captured, but the "fear factor increased" when Cavalcante shaved and changed his appearance. The residents wondered, "What does he look like now?"

The homeowner's association issued alerts. One posted on the community's Facebook page on September 7 was especially frightening. "TAL [Traditions at Longwood] residents please make sure All your OUTDOOR LIGHTS are ON & DOORS & WINDOWS LOCKED. Perimeter for the man hunt shifted towards you today."

Replies to the Facebook posting included "*NOW* I'm kinda nervous, but all locked up, all lights on." Another response was "Oh ok! Scary situation." Some residents did more than turn on lights and locked doors. One said he slept with his handgun.

The September 7 alert was tied to a sighting at nearby Longwood Gardens. Pennsylvania State Police patrol cars were parked at the entrance to the development. The guarding trooper told residents they were making a show of force but didn't know exactly where Cavalcante was hiding. "We are just letting him know we are out here," the trooper was quoted as saying.

Two days after the Facebook alert, a resident said her family went out to do some much-needed shopping. The road was clear, but when they returned an hour later, Route 926 was lined with police vehicles, and the officers had their guns drawn.

During the manhunt, both Conley and his wife, Kathy, walked their dog. Previously, just one of them did so. "It was unnerving," one resident commented. Another said it was "very scary" and was reluctant to go out of her home, since Cavalcante could have been there. An eighty-year-old resident said, "That was the first time in my life that I feared for my well-being." Another commented, "The longer the search continued, the more concerned I became. He [Cavalcante] must be becoming more desperate."

The fear didn't stop all activities at Traditions at Longwood. A planned holiday pool party took place. "We didn't believe he [Cavalcante] would come to our gathering," a resident said.

Once Cavalcante was captured, the thought of an escaped murderer in their midst didn't subside. "We all gave out a big sigh of relief," one community member said. "We want to get back to our normal lives. We are getting there, but in the back of our minds we wonder about our safety."

CHAPTER 9

FEAR AND NAIVETY

As fear enveloped Pocopson, across the region, nation, and world, people followed the plight of the terrified community.

In an article in *USA Today* by writer David Oliver on the Cavalcante escape, Oliver posed this question: "Why did this news captivate the nation?" Oliver continued, "Much like the *Titanic* submersible tragedy earlier this year, people can't help but doom scroll their lives away. Experts caution that fear will always be around us—but it doesn't mean it has to hold us back."

On June 18, 2023, the *Titan*, a submersible owned by the American company OceanGate, imploded during an expedition to view the wreck of the *Titanic* off the coast of Newfoundland. Five people were on the *Titan*. For four days, world news organizations gave updates on the search for the missing crew and passengers. They all are believed to have died shortly after beginning the ill-fated dive.

"It's understandable to fear the unknown; no one walks around with their hands over their eyes for a reason," Raquel Martin, licensed clinical psychologist, was quoted as saying in Oliver's article. "But when that fear stops you from engaging with the world, then there is an issue."

Some of the Pocopson residents did stop engaging with the world. Trips to the food store and necessary visits to pharmacies were delayed for days. Students were kept from their studies and their friends as they stayed in their homes. Some made their houses an armed fortress.

Chester County therapist Charlene Briggs wrote about her experiences during the escape. "It was impossible to sleep," Briggs recalled. "I remember staying up late glued to news feeds night after night, watching the perimeter of his location move from where my friends lived to where I lived." She recalled the "incessant hum" of the searching helicopters.

The unknown was frightening. Briggs continued, "How did an international murderer wind up on the loose for two weeks in our backyards? People saw him lurking in their woods. Innocent children waved to him. Dogs announced his presence. Parents rushed home to their families only to be prevented from entering their neighborhoods while their partners, caregivers, and children were trapped inside their homes on lockdown. No one on his trail was safe for what felt like an eternity, while images of a man who stabbed his girlfriend thirty-seven times in front of her children cut through our nights like a dagger."

Oliver wrote, "You likely played out sickening scenarios in your head: What would I do if the gunman arrived at my doorstep? Could I outsmart him and help turn him in to the authorities? Would I be brave enough? But we can never be prepared for a situation like this until we're confronted with it."

The article added comments by Regine Galanti, a clinical psychologist. Galanti wrote, "We're scared of what we don't know precisely because we don't know how bad it can turn out, so we imagine the worst, and we hyperfixate on that danger until it is resolved, in theory, so we can be prepared for it and see it coming. In practice, it means we doom scroll, and it doesn't get us any more prepared because there's nothing an everyday person can do about an escaped murderer. There's an evolutionary benefit to this—people who think the worst are more prepared. The person who is constantly at the doctor for every mole will be more likely to detect skin cancer, and the person who keeps their eye on the escaped convict would, in theory, be more prepared."

For the most part, the community gathered together and supported each other and the law enforcement officials combing the hinterlands of Chester County for the escaped murderer. Having Cavalcante loose in the county was a jolt to county residents.

Briggs continued, "How could this happen in Chester County, a bucolic landscape graced with fresh air, farms, and forests intersecting with suburbia? Safe, connected communities and exceptional schools drew many of us to this county; the wealthiest per capita county in the state and one of the wealthiest in the nation. We are populated by well-educated professionals, highly skilled laborers, hardworking farmers, business leaders, entrepreneurs, social advocates, and many active faith-based communities. Our police forces are some of the best trained in the nation.

"But we were not smart enough to prevent or expeditiously circumvent a perfect storm. Starting with a prison guard absorbed in a game on his phone while a convicted murderer scaled prison walls, ignition keys poised in a farm van waiting to be stolen, an accessible suburban home stocked with survival supplies casually ransacked, with terrified parents and children upstairs and a loaded gun just inside an open garage door. This story would barely be plausible if it was fiction."

The story was real, not a piece of Hollywood fiction, to the residents.

The community was not immediately healed when Cavalcante was captured. The pain may never heal. "I have seen how the resonance of trauma lives on in the internal landscape long after the traumatic event ends in the external landscape," Briggs wrote. One grandfather wrote that his grandson, months after the Cavalcante escape concluded, was traumatized every time he heard a helicopter or was reminded of the murderer's escape from prison.

Youngsters weren't the only persons having frightening flashbacks. Adults admitted to the same feelings.

Randy Mims, who lived in Pocopson for twenty-five years before the escape, was present when Norman Johnston escaped and roamed the area. "I remember some helicopters searching for Johnston, but not like the Cavalcante search. This was constant. I remember the voice of Cavalcante's mother being broadcast, asking for her son to surrender. Several months after his capture, a bad traffic accident took place nearby. A helicopter was summoned to help the injured party. I remember flinching when I heard the helicopter. I can relate to PTSD."

Posttraumatic stress disorder (PTSD) is defined as a disorder that develops when a person has experienced or witnessed a scary, shocking, terrifying, or dangerous event. These stressful or traumatic events usually involve a situation where someone's life has been threatened or severe injury has occurred.

A Kennett resident was alarmed by helicopters, long after Cavalcante was captured. She asked on Facebook on Halloween, "Anyone else hearing all the helicopters? Do we know why?"

While the majority of residents heeded internal survival instincts and stayed as far away from the convicted murderer as possible, some left common sense at the door of their homes. Did they believe the search was some sort of computer game? One disaffected set was the gawkers.

As social media wannabe reporters broadcast from search sites—all the broadcast hunts were futile—spectators gathered on lawn chairs to watch heavily armed law enforcement officers delve into the woods and underbrush. Some even brought alcoholic drinks for the show. Families were seen with their children frolicking nearby.

One Traditions at Longwood resident returned home on a Friday evening during the search. For a treat during the long siege, he vacated the safety of his community to go for a pizza for his family. When he returned, he noticed a gaggle of cars parked in his neighborhood. "Some of the travelers were out across the way with cocktails, watching. Cars were parked everywhere. They had children with them. What did they think they were going to see? Did they want their children to see someone shot?"

Several persons interviewed for this book likened the response of alcohol-sipping voyagers to spectators at the first major battle of the Civil War, Manassas. Residents and politicians from Washington, DC, ventured outside the confines of the city with picnic lunches and opera glasses to view the fighting. The battle on July 21, 1861, was also known as Bull Run. Men, women, and children were among the spectators. Congressmen were front and center for the action that some later labeled the "picnic battle."

Union captain John Tidball recorded he saw a "throng of sightseers" near his position. Tidball described a crowd eager to watch the battle. "It was Sunday, and everybody seemed to have taken a general holiday," he wrote. The soldier reported that when the battle concluded and the Union army had been routed, he retreated to

Washington along with several US senators. Another report had spectators scrambling for carriages. "Carriages collided, tearing away wheels; then horses were cut loose and ridden without saddles."

The fear of the Confederate cavalry chasing the Union army kept everyone hurrying toward Washington. Some of the picnickers, including a legislator, were captured by Southern forces and imprisoned in Richmond, Virginia. What the gawkers witnessed on their Sunday outing was more than eight hundred men killed and another 4,200 soldiers wounded or missing.

Another person interviewed for this book said the behavior reminded him of reports of people gathering to watch public hangings and beheadings.

The public turned out again to line the roadside of Route 926 after Cavalcante was captured. Residents of Traditions at Longwood gathered at the end of Primrose Drive. They believed that the law enforcement escort would pass them as they transported Cavalcante to the Pennsylvania State Police barracks in Avondale. The residents planned to wave goodbye to the escaped murderer who caused so much havoc in their lives. The residents were disappointed. The motorcade turned before passing Primrose Drive.

Chester County psychotherapist Michele Paiva commented, "I was both observing and experiencing a rollercoaster of emotions. As the summer drew to a close, myself and other residents were thrust into a state of lockdown, our lives forever altered by the escape of a notorious murderer, because crisis and trauma always change us. Fear, anxiety, and frustration became daily companions, for all, reshaping lives in profound ways."

Not everyone was thrilled to see Cavalcante captured.

Paiva reported conversations by women saying the murderer who stabbed his girlfriend to death was cute and they would invite him to their homes. Others were openly rooting for Cavalcante to continue to avoid capture. They were rooting for the diminutive underdog. The same behavior was seen during the hunt for murderer Norman Johnston in 1999; "*Run Norm Run*" shirts were produced.

"That just shows a lack of maturity," Kennett resident Brian Sprowal said of those comments and responses.

Nancy Brill and her daughter Sharon Maxwell of Downingtown gave some insights into the initial support voiced for Cavalcante. Brill mentioned that Cavalcante had issues he shared with the police officers chasing him. "It was hot; he must have been uncomfortable, especially hiding in the brush with deer ticks and prickers," Brill said. "Did he have a pillowcase with him?"

At first, Brill said she wasn't too concerned, since Cavalcante, to her, was "just another criminal." When Brill first heard reports of some Chester County schools closing because of an escaped prisoner, she thought school district officials were overreacting. "Why were they so worried?"

During a family Labor Day picnic, Brill had a conversation with her brother-in-law. "I hope they get that murderer," the family member told Brill. "I wasn't aware of the facts surrounding the murder," Brill said. "I wasn't following the media or the social media."

Later during the search, Brill admitted being fearful. "I was walking my dog near the Brandywine [river]. I thought he [Cavalcante] could be out there. He could have followed the Brandywine to my location."

During the search, Brill said she did check news reports, just to see if Cavalcante had been captured. She also made sure her home and car were locked at all times. Brill wasn't totally afraid, since she believed he wasn't a serial killer, like Ted Bundy. "He killed a person in a relationship," Brill said. Bundy admitted to murdering thirty women during the 1970s.

Brill was in California when Cavalcante was captured. "One of my coworkers alerted me," Brill said. "I then watched the reports on television."

Members of Generation Z identified with Cavalcante, according to Maxwell, herself a member of the Zoomers, as Generation Z is sometimes known. Maxwell was attending Thomas Jefferson University during the search for Cavalcante.

"My friends and I are interested in the *Hunger Games*, reality shows, survivalists, *Alone*, true crime, and Jeffrey Dahmer," Maxwell said. She said the "crab-walking" escape was an attraction to her friends. "Crab walking is part of the ninja warrior training," she said.

The wisdom of the bounty hunters is questionable. There was a danger of being in the woods and fields of Pocopson with other armed civilians. Firearm training, if the civilian bounty seekers possessed any, was unknown. The bounty hunters very well could have shot each other, as a number of law enforcement officers pointed out during interviews. Despite the dangers, the thrill of the peril and the lure of the reward money enticed many, near and far, to take up arms and attempt to capture Cavalcante.

Did they consider the desperate prey they were seeking? Cavalcante was facing a lifetime in prison for murder. He was charged with a second murder. He was armed, first with a knife and later with a rifle. Cavalcante had nothing to lose by killing another person.

"There is a lot more to this than running with a gun and saying come out," one Traditions at Longwood resident commented.

While law enforcement gathered information, made plans, and coordinated movements of the highly armed investigators, not so for the bounty hunters. They responded to reported sightings by social media bloggers and plunged into the woods.

During the search, Police Chief Martinez said, some people appeared on four-wheelers and wanted to capture Cavalcante for the reward. "We told them to leave the area," Martinez said. In his own West Caln Township, miles from where Cavalcante was credibly seen, "seven or eight false sightings" were reported, according to Martinez.

Pennsbury Township resident Amy Dettore related her observations of a neighbor. She called him "Mr. Macho." At one point in the search, Cavalcante was reportedly sighted on Chandler Road in the Dettores' neighborhood. There is some question if Cavalcante was ever near Chandler Road, since it is east of Longwood Gardens, near the elementary school and Ace Hardware store. From confirmed sightings, Cavalcante would have had to travel east to the area of the hardware store and then backtrack the same distance to the area of Longwood Gardens where he was later seen.

Dettore saw a man walking in a pasture going into the woods in the back of her home. The man was armed with a rifle. Dettore wasn't sure if the man was a police officer, Cavalcante, or a civilian. In time, she realized the person was Mr. Macho. "Two days later I saw him doing the same thing," Dettore said. "Within ten minutes, police cruisers were pulling into our street. The officers were putting on their vests and gathering their equipment from the trunks of cars. I talked with them, and I told them I believed the man was our neighbor."

The police packed up their gear and returned to the command center.

Joe Dettore, Amy's husband, said they encountered bounty hunters on their land. "They drove onto our property," Joe Dettore said. "We yelled at them; it was the vigilante guys coming up in cars. They told me they were looking for the reward money. I told them to get out. They made us mad. Having them around was the last thing we needed."

Pocopson resident Judy Love reported that at one point she yelled at the bounty chasers to leave her property.

Kathryn Humpfry of Beversrede Trail believes she had a bizarre encounter with a bounty hunter. She commented that she said she couldn't be sure the mother and son were seeking the reward, since they don't have "bounty hunter" stamped on their foreheads. On Sunday afternoon, three days after the escape, she saw a state police car posted at the end of her driveway. She then saw a car that definitely was not from her neighborhood. Humpfry deemed the situation odd. The unknown car left and then returned.

"A woman was sitting in her car, and I asked if she was okay," Humpfry related. "She said she and her son were visiting friends. She couldn't tell me anything about the friend. Then she said that she and her son were watching a social media broadcast and wanted to come and help with the search. Her son claimed he had found a blanket and a can in the area, and they reported the find to a police officer. I spoke to the police officer. The son and mother were from Phoenixville. The police officer said he collected a blanket. The son had peed on the blanket in case Cavalcante was using it, to make the murderer angry."

Humpfry wondered if the son marked the blanket just in case it was being used by Cavalcante and the blanket was used to facilitate the murderer's capture. The son could have claimed the reward since he had a DNA connection to the evidence

After the lockdown lifted from her street, Humpfry said gawkers were up and down the road.

Not all the non-law-enforcement searches were done by lone bounty hunters and mother-and-son teams. A group vigilante outing was organized. Armed community members were to meet at the Ace Hardware store, near the search zone. A notification was posted on the township's Facebook page and quickly deleted. Some people did show up at the appointed hour at Ace. No mass civilian search was amassed that day.

Facebook posters were anxious and critical. One wrote a caution for neighbors on the Pocopson page. It read: "For me, it's important to remember that if we're hearing helicopters and still seeing a lot of state troopers, there is still a serious risk, and we should act responsibly. Pointing fingers and coming up with brilliant ideas on how things could be done better. At this moment, those thought processes are non-effective or productive. After this is over, we can all collectively put our thoughts to paper and submit them responsibly to Chester county commissioners to start and stay on it until we get meaningful actions in writing. We are not hearing anything more because they have nothing to say. They don't know where he is, and I'm sure the minute he is caught it'll be on every news station; if it's during office hours, the township will notify us, Chesco will notify us, because they'll be so happy to have him in custody. This guy is no joke."

District Attorney Ryan said the bounty hunters caused investigators problems. For all the good done by the reward-chasing bounty hunters, they should have left the hunt to the trained law enforcement officers.

CHAPTER 10

PROOF OF LIFE

While the gawkers, bounty hunters, and social media followers were chasing every reported sighting of Danilo Cavalcante across Chester County and neighboring communities, the trained investigators concentrated on "proof of life" evidence. Verified sightings—the proof-of-life evidence—weren't easy to attain.

"A lot of tips were called in, and I believe everyone was trying to be helpful," Clark, supervisory deputy of the US Marshals Service, said. "Some were look-alike tips. I only believed what I saw on video cameras. We were concentrating on where he was going. How could we get ahead of him?"

What Clark most believed came from trail cams, and video footage from commercial and private homes, including Ring's video doorbell monitoring system. "We were relieved when we had the first trail cam sighting," Clark said. "We knew he was still in the area."

The trail cams were so important, especially on property at Longwood Gardens where Cavalcante migrated, that law enforcement utilized everyone immediately available to them and purchased additional video devices. The cameras were keeping a silent and watchful eye on Cavalcante. Some of the original cams were owned by Longwood Gardens, and others were placed on the property, with the approval of the Longwood management, by individuals.

"Time and again he [Cavalcante] was caught on the trail cams," Clark said. "We wanted immediate access to the video, so we could watch live. That wasn't possible, and we were getting information twelve hours old in some cases."

As trail cam footage was analyzed and other information evaluated, law enforcement adjusted the perimeters of their searches. New neighborhoods and roads were blocked with each new boundary. For more than a week, law enforcement believed that Cavalcante was wandering aimlessly in the vicinity of the prison and Longwood Gardens. The murderer wasn't familiar with the area.

The first video sighting of Cavalcante came two hours after the burglary of the Drummond home. Video from a residential surveillance camera recorded the murderer in the 1800 block of Lenape Road at 1:43 a.m. on Saturday. Cavalcante was seen emerging from behind a small tree and wearing a backpack.

The videotape was released to the public later in the morning. "We are confident that if he is in there, we will find him," Bivens said during the Labor Day afternoon press conference in the Chester County Government Services building.

"We're asking for the public's help in a number of ways," Bivens told the public, including having residents familiarize themselves with Cavalcante's description and photograph. The citizens were asked to stay away from the wooded areas, check on their neighbors, and report to troopers if homes were vacant because of the Labor Day weekend. Another request was for residents to check security cameras in case Cavalcante was pictured.

"We're not trying to lock people down; we just want to keep them as safe as possible while we thoroughly search that area," Bivens told reporters.

The press conference was vastly different than the first one on the day of the escape. Clark, who represented the Marshal's Service, said only three news reporters attended the initial press briefing. That all changed when Cavalcante's crab-walking video was posted. "We went from a local news story barely being covered to an international sensation," Clark said. A horde of reporters seemed to appear out of nowhere. Clark and Bivens dealt with a roomful of reporters, others falsely claiming to be reporters, and social media sleuths, some demanding immediate answers to bogus sightings and nonsensical theories, for the duration of the search.

To alleviate some of the second-guessing of law enforcement's investigative techniques by the public and distrust by the media, at one point Bivens invited reporters to tour the command facility at Po-Mar-Lin firehouse. The unusual offer to see firsthand the workings of an ongoing investigation eliminated some of the questions from reporters and the public. One investigator said the decision to allow the press to have an inside glimpse was brilliant.

When Cavalcante was seen within a mile of Longwood Gardens, the tourist attraction closed for the day. The gardens barred visitors for several days for the search. The Brandywine Museum of Art in Chadds Ford, another popular tourist destination, decided to remain open. Later, the museum closed because of the Cavalcante hunt.

Later in the day, Bivens reported that a Pennsylvania state trooper reported seeing Cavalcante in the Longwood area.

Longwood posed several issues for the law enforcement seekers. Longwood was in the midst of major construction, reported to cost $250 million. The new West Conservatory was a year away from the projected opening when Cavalcante fled. Construction equipment and material were scattered throughout the site. Cases of bottled water were available for the construction workers, and thus for the escaped murderer. A tunnel system providing access for workers to service the gardens and be hidden from the sight of visitors covered parts of the attraction. There were plenty of places for Cavalcante to hide and fresh water to be had.

On Sunday, hundreds of law enforcement officers joined the search for Cavalcante. Police Chief Martinez recalled Sunday as being very hot. His K-9, Matrix, went down with heat exhaustion and was throwing up. Martinez called his vet, and Matrix was treated and fully recovered.

The teams searched fields near and distant from Chester County Prison, concentrating on the Longwood Gardens area. Officials reported to the public that four credible sightings of the at-large murderer had been made. While these were credible, police were still relying on proof-of-life sightings.

Sophisticated surveillance gear, including heat-identifying systems in airplanes, was utilized without success. "It was superhot," Clark said. "The area was super overgrown. He had so many hiding spots. People thought the heat system could see through things. That's not true. It doesn't work like that. You need to have a direct line of sight to the object. The system won't cut through canopies. We had some sightings that turned out to be a deer standing against a tree. If the time of the year was winter with less foliage, the search would have been a lot easier."

The FBI's first search was with a Pennsylvania State Police tactical team, according to Milligan. They responded to a possible sighting around a creek bed. "The first few days we didn't have confirmed sightings," Milligan said. "He then was spotted near the northern edge of Longwood Gardens." The FBI's Tactical Operation Center unit had joined the command post at Po-Mar-Lin Fire Company. The tactical team consulted maps and decided to conduct a massive search of Longwood. "I didn't appreciate how rugged the terrain was," Milligan said. "We have a system to keep track of our guys. They were moving so slow. The terrain was far more rugged than the area where we looked for Frein. "The Longwood area was so thick with brambles, one of our men said he got stuck in a bush and was suspended off the ground. It was a tough area. I didn't have an appreciation of how rugged it was. I thought of Longwood Gardens as a botanical amusement park. It wasn't. Also, it was really hot, and we had heat casualties."

One member of the law enforcement team was a volunteer, Constable Bill Carozzo, who worked out of the office of district judge Matthew Seavey of Kennett Square. Carozzo said he believed that Cavalcante had an advantage over the large search teams and sophisticated technology. The dense undergrowth, briars, bamboo, and storm tunnels gave the escaped murderer plenty of places to hide, according to Carozzo. "There could have been six hundred of us out there searching, and he would still have had the advantage. With the heat, the dogs were good for only ten or fifteen minutes at a time. At one point, I counted fifteen dogs from Pennsylvania, Delaware, and Maryland."

For ten days, Carozzo patrolled the perimeter of the search around Longwood Gardens. "I was hot, and I was tired," Carozzo said. "My job as a constable is to search for people. Finding [Cavalcante] became an obsession. It was becoming personal for many of us."

Carozzo's obsession led him to purchase his own night-vision equipment and to keep watch over a field at Longwood Gardens. His surveillance went a little too far during one early morning. "I ventured out into the field and then into the middle of some woods. I'm out there with my AR [automatic rifle], and I realized I could be mistaken for Cavalcante. I stopped my solo searches."

On the Pocopson Facebook page on September 4, Judy Love posted, "Another day is here and the jerk's not caught. I'd like to remind people that many of our residents have been locked down not able to leave. I'm sure frustrations are rising fast[,] which we can all understand and sympathize with. That said[,] if anyone there would like to comment if you need anything please comment here. Could people from Waterglen and Parker[s]ville let me know if you're still locked down? If you are and we can get supplies to you, we will do our best. Everyone has been great considering the stress levels. Please if people get a bit sparky don't take to heart[;] people are highly stressed right now. I'm so proud of our community right now. Remember only confirmed things will be posted [on the township Facebook page]. Stay safe[;] remember he can be anywhere at this point. A comment: one of the planes is a homeland security plane[,] a Pilalus 12 Spectre with sophisticated machinery."

By Labor Day, Monday, September 4, law enforcement had additional confirmed sightings of Cavalcante. Twice the runaway murderer was seen on cameras. The first footage showed the murderer walking north, toward the prison, at 8:21 p.m. The second sighting of Cavalcante was at 9:33 p.m. with the fugitive heading south. Clearly visible on the videos were a backpack, a type of a duffel bag, and a hooded sweatshirt.

Police believed that Cavalcante was hiding in a wooded area of Pocopson Township bordered by the intersection of Routes 926 and 52 (where the Karco convenience store is located), and north to Parkersville Road. The perimeter included the Drummond home. On Tuesday, another possible sighting, this time by a resident in nearby Pennsbury Township, placed Cavalcante in a creek bed near Chandler Road. The person fled into the woods before police arrived. A futile search lasted hours, according to Bivens.

A member of one of the three special quick-response teams described his experiences during the searches. "When the state police set up a perimeter, we had teams ready at the Karco or other locations. When we were asked to check homes, we'd go in teams of two or four and clear the residence. At times our game plan was to sit and wait for him to pop out of bushes. We had drones and helicopters searching at night. We used flashlights and night-vision goggles to do our big pushes. One night, we did a big push with all the park rangers and fugitive task force members, and we got in a line. He was spotted by a creek bed, and we lined up in the backyard and pushed through the woods. We never saw him. We were looking for signs of a person there, but the area had been searched so much, with all of the footprints we couldn't tell who was who.

"During some of the searches, state police cars with red and blue lights on were in the road, and their headlights were pointed at the car in front of them and not at the wood line. With all the blinking lights and being out all night, it harms night vision. It was a major flaw."

The searcher said he was involved in a number of searches, including one of the railroad tracks near the elementary school. He said his team had another duty: keeping the bounty hunters out of the perimeter.

"I'm quite confident we're wearing him down," Bivens told reporters.

The Chandler Road sighting was never verified, and some people believe it was a false sighting.

The movement of the police perimeter brought law enforcement to the residence of former Chester County sheriff Carolyn "Bunny" Welsh's home in Pennsbury Township. She lives 6 miles from the prison. "They were in my front yard," she commented. "We had an RV, and they needed to check it. They were searching everywhere. It was quite a sight to see ten cars, helicopters, and guys with ARs [automatic rifles] outside my home."

For Randy Mims, law enforcement never visited his Pocopson Township home, even though it is 1.5 miles from the prison. The route to his home from the prison is a straight line through a greenway. Mims lives in a hollow, and during the summer, one can't see very far into the woods.

The property includes a barn and a guesthouse. They were unlocked when Cavalcante made his getaway. Mims and his wife conducted their own search of the structures.

On Wednesday, additional resources were added to the search. The FBI and the US Border Patrol became involved. Another adjustment of the perimeter was made as the boundary moved to the east toward the Brandywine River. The far end included an elementary school and an Ace Hardware store. Adding to the traffic chaos caused by the blocked roads was a freight train line that runs along the Brandywine. With the police checkpoints, Route 926 was jammed with more-than-usual traffic when the train crossed the road.

During the daily press conference, information was disclosed to the public about Cavalcante's escape, and additional footage from the prison was made available to the public. Also, for the first time officials confirmed to the public that Cavalcante escaped from the same place and in the same way as prisoner Bolte did a few weeks before Cavalcante.

Acting warden Howard Holland, during the press conference, commented, "We know the gravity of the situation and how it has impacted the community significantly. The victims of this individual's crimes remain in our thoughts and prayers as we work to bring him to justice." Holland declined to answer several queries from the press, including details of the escape and if Cavalcante had any assistance in the planning of his escape.

As Thursday dawned, Bivens believed that the schools were safe to reopen, and they did so that day. The search had moved east toward the Brandywine River and Creek Road and away from Longwood Gardens. Longwood Gardens reopened for business but kept its expansive 86-acre Meadow Garden closed. The Meadow Garden offered enticing hiding places for Cavalcante.

Police were paying attention to the fields at Longwood. Jamie Hicks, who farms the Longwood land, was enlisted to cut a field to make sure Cavalcante wasn't hiding there.

He remembers the ominous police presence guarding the operation as he worked and later being left alone with the helicopters. Several deer jumped up, but no escaped murderer. Hicks said the field was thick enough to hide in and not be seen. A milk protein bottle was found near a pond, and Hicks believes it could have been discarded by Cavalcante.

The Unionville–Chadds Ford School District gave parents a warning on Thursday. "Rapid changes may occur to secure an area, so please pay attention and be vigilant."

A rapid change was about to take place.

Another proof-of-life sighting, a trail camera image of Cavalcante near Longwood Gardens, was recorded on Wednesday evening. Because of the delay in processing images, police were not alerted until Thursday afternoon. One week after his escape, Cavalcante was within a mile of the prison and only a half mile from where another camera captured him on Monday.

Again, Cavalcante was sighted in a wooded area near Longwood Gardens on Thursday. The murderer was glimpsed about noon. After being alerted, Longwood Gardens closed early and people on the property were ordered to shelter in place. Longwood added extra security and contracted with East Marlborough Township to have its officers provide extra coverage, one law enforcement officer said. An extensive search by a large contingent of state police troopers took place on the garden grounds and of barns and outbuildings near Longwood. Mounted state police troopers on horseback took part in the search. Also, drones were utilized in the hunt for Cavalcante.

During a press conference on Thursday afternoon, Bivens said, "This is an amazing operation going on here. This is not a situation where we have a police dispatcher sitting and waiting for calls to come in. Searchers have gone to that area. We're using people on foot. We have horses out there as well that are assisting with the search." He added that tactical teams were being aided by "aviation assets": the drones, airplanes, and ever-present helicopters.

A voice from the sky was part of law enforcement's aviation arsenal. The voice was that of Cavalcante's mother imploring her son to surrender. Clark interviewed Eleni Cavalcante, sister of the escaped murderer. Clark requested that Eleni obtain the message from her mother, Iracema Cavalcante. The sister indicated she would do so and later in the day talked with her mother. Eleni Cavalcante captured Iracema Cavalcante's plea on her cell phone. The recording was forwarded to Clark. Several Brazilian translators reviewed the message, and eventually the plea was broadcast from a helicopter's public-address system.

The mother's plea was repeatedly broadcast to Cavalcante and heard by already fearful Chester County residents. Joe Dettore clearly remembers the message from the helicopter. "Everybody was on edge," Dettore said. "Roads were shut down; kids were scared, and we were within earshot of the helicopter with his mother speaking in Portuguese."

Later, Cavalcante reported hearing his mother's voice. Her plea didn't entice him to surrender.

The possible sightings of Cavalcante, Bivens indicated, fell within the perimeter of the search zone that police previously established, which covered about 8 to 10 square miles. That perimeter remained largely unchanged, with the exception of two schools, Greenwood Elementary and Chadds Ford Elementary, being removed from the search zone, according to Bivens.

A woman visiting Longwood Gardens told a reporter for the *Philadelphia Inquirer* that she was about to leave the gardens when she was asked to go into the lobby and shelter in place. The woman, who declined to be identified, lived in Chadds Ford and worked nearby the gardens. She said a Longwood staff person told them they were being sheltered because of a nearby storm. "No one was really buying that," she told the reporter. "It's been stressful for our community."

The visitors stayed in the lobby for only a few minutes. Another staff person told them to go to their cars and vacate Longwood immediately for their safety. The Chadds Ford woman did so. A Longwood Gardens spokesperson commented Thursday night that the shelter-in-place order was still in effect as law enforcement searched the grounds for escaped prisoner Danilo Cavalcante.

Patricia Evans, a spokesperson for Longwood Gardens, issued an email at 8:15 p.m. It read, "In cooperation with authorities, we have closed the gardens and cleared the property of guests. Police are currently searching an area of interest on the property. Tenants on the property are sheltering in place. The Gardens will remain closed until further notice."

As did Longwood Gardens, the Brandywine Museum of Art safeguarded visitors. "We took all necessary steps to ensure the safety of our visitors, volunteers, and staff throughout the search. We were also in touch daily with local law enforcement and followed their guidance," said Nicole Kindbeiter, director of marketing and communications. No specific details were disclosed, since the museum doesn't provide details about the security procedures and precautions in place.

Next to Longwood Gardens sits a historic Society of Friends (the Quakers) meetinghouse. The building is used by the Chester County Conference and Visitors Bureau to promote Chester County's rich historic and cultural attractions, including Longwood Gardens and the Brandywine Museum of Art. While the business of marketing Chester County did not stop during the search for Cavalcante, the meetinghouse office itself was closed and staff members worked remotely.

As the search began its second week, law enforcement was convinced they were closing in on Cavalcante. The amount of time taken to capture the diminutive Brazilian murderer was wearing on the public, but Bivens indicated the search teams were undaunted. They were convinced the murderer would be captured despite formidable challenges, including the heat, the humidity, and the expansive rugged territory.

"We've chased people for a lot longer than this and ultimately brought them to justice," Bivens commented during one press conference. "As I've said before, we're not going anywhere. We will eventually capture him. And when we do, he's going to prison."

Bivens made the statement after a reporter shouted a question implying that Cavalcante was "winning" in his effort to remain free.

One such extensive hunt was for Eric Frein, convicted of murdering Pennsylvania state trooper Bryon K. Dickson and wounding trooper Alex Douglass on September 12, 2014. The search took forty-eight days and cost taxpayers an estimated $12 million. Frein was captured on October 30, 2014. He was taken into custody after being found by members of the US Marshals Service.

Ironically, Chester County was involved in the trial of Frein. In June 2016, judges determined that too much prejudicial publicity was circulating in Pike County. A jury from Chester County would decide Frein's fate. Jury selection took place in the Chester County Justice Center in West Chester. The justice center housed the offices of the sheriff, district attorney, and county detectives involved in the Cavalcante search. Frein was transported to Chester County for jury selection by members of the Chester County Sheriff's Office, then under the direction of Welsh. Frein was convicted of murder and sentenced to death.

Cavalcante's capture and incarceration couldn't come soon enough for the members of the public. One resident, James Cleare, commented to a reporter, "It's a slap in the face, and it feels like it's up to us to decide to move from the place where another guy could hop a fence and be in our backyard, in eye line of our daughter. I respect law enforcement like anyone else, but with every press conference it's just 'Keep your eyes peeled,' never mind that [the murderer] is getting more desperate."

Cleare had a good reason to be upset. When Igor Bolte escaped from Chester County Prison on May 19, 2023, Cleare's backyard security camera recorded the escaped convict. Bolte was on a walking trail about a half mile from the prison. Cleare and his wife, Jenna, alerted prison officials, and Bolte was captured.

The main concentration of resources remained in an 8-square-mile area of Longwood Gardens. The position of the net spread by the police appeared to be correct, since two additional sightings took place on Friday. Almost four hundred law enforcement members from local, state, and federal agencies, including the DEA (Drug Enforcement Administration), reportedly joined the search that day.

Certainly, the officials of the nearby Kennett Square community had faith that Cavalcante would be captured. The manhunt wasn't about to curtail the thirty-ninth annual Mushroom Festival, held that weekend. Kennett Square fancies itself the Mushroom Capital of the World. Every year, according to the festival committee, thousands of people gather during the two-day event "to sample a variety of mushroom-centric foods, from fried mushrooms to mushroom soup and many other dishes and learn about mystical and interesting process of mushroom growing."

The latest search perimeter didn't include Kennett Square, the state police assured festival organizers. Also, no one expected a hunted murderer to mingle with the mushroom crowds. While nearby, Cavalcante didn't attend the mushroom festival, or at least no one recognized him.

CHAPTER 11

ESCAPING THE PERIMETER

While fungus lovers had their fill of mushrooms at the Kennett Square festival on Saturday, September 9, Cavalcante was moving and eluding detection by law enforcement. The murderer kept to the treelines of the expansive search area bordering Longwood Gardens, seeking a way to escape his hunters. He was obtaining water and food, including watermelons from local farmers, but sustenance was becoming difficult to obtain. He later told police he thought about giving up several times during the search.

Cavalcante moved mainly at night. During his Saturday evening wanderings, he discovered an opportunity he was seeking. He made his way off Longwood property to the north and west. Cavalcante needed transportation to put miles between him and his pursuing posse. His final destination wasn't known, but later Cavalcante indicated that Canada or a return to Puerto Rico and then Brazil were possibilities.

Neighbors were afraid the murderer would try to carjack one of them and harm family members in the process. No violence was needed by Cavalcante to secure his ride.

A commonsense message was repeatedly broadcast to residents during the search: "Be vigilant and keep your doors and cars locked." Clark recalled a warning issued by Bivens. "He told residents to make sure you secure your property, as the last thing we wanted to see was him getting a vehicle and getting out of the perimeter. That is what exactly took place," Clark said.

Close to the perimeter boundary enforced on Saturday evening, but not inside the boundary, was a popular dairy. Products were sold, including ice cream, milk, brown eggs, cheese, and seasonal produce. The farm, located near the prison on Lenape Unionville Road, is used for children's birthday parties. Sisters Becky Baily and Meredith Parsons, the owners of Baily's Dairy on Pocopson Meadow Farm, supported community initiatives. The farm has been identified as being in the Baily family since the 1800s.

The search for Cavalcante had disrupted the operation of the farm and cost them income. "We closed the farm market for several days," Parsons said. "We did have milk for customers, as it was self-service. We canceled birthday parties. We continued our farm chores; we had no choice. This is our life. It was exhausting."

Saturday night was the first night that Parsons had a good sleep in a week. "We thought the search was over. Police were searching Longwood. We were led to believe he was about to be captured. Our farm wasn't within the police search perimeter. There were no helicopters circling the farm," she said. "Before that, they [helicopters] were constant. Having the helicopters constantly circling was the worst part of the search. Today, when I see a helicopter, I wonder what is going on."

Parsons and the farmworkers were careful during the week. "We let down our guard once," Parsons said. "Looking back, all of us would make different choices.

"We have fourteen vehicles registered here, plus tractors. If he knew anything about mechanics or how to jump-start a car, he would have taken a vehicle even if the van's keys weren't in the van. [Cavalcante] was a good criminal. He took the newest vehicle, which was a break. It had the latest tracking devices."

On Saturday, the Bailys went about their daily work routine. A morning delivery was made using the farm's delivery van. The vehicle was then parked behind a shed in the rear of the property. Parsons remembered seeing the van at 6:00 p.m. The workday, even with a convicted murderer on the loose in the area, didn't change.

That evening the farmworkers were unaware that Cavalcante was across the road from the farm, watching their every move. After a period, Cavalcante managed to cross the road unseen. He silently crept to the barn. The murderer later told police that he found keys in the visor of a 2020 white Ford transit van.

"I was still on the farm about 8:00 p.m.," Parsons said. "There are lots of vehicles on the property, and some of our employees take a vehicle home at night. I didn't notice the van wasn't there."

The Bailys posted a note on Facebook: "Friends—Our delivery van was stolen last night between 7:00–10:00 p.m. while we were still here working. It is believed that Cavalcante used it to flee the Pocopson area. We are still working with LE to help with the investigation. We really do not have any other information at this time and are just as disappointed as everyone that he broke through the perimeter in Longwood. We appreciate the support of the community and continuing efforts of Law Enforcement."

The Bailys received criticism on social media for leaving the keys in the vehicle. One person wondered why keys were left in vehicles at any time with the prison so close. Parsons said, "The first few days we had calls and letters and hate mail. None were signed. The communications came mostly from out of state, some from the DC area."

The surrounding community was sympathetic. Parsons said, "We have not seen any drop-off in support for the store or us, actually the opposite. The community support after initial shock was outstanding. We never skipped a beat with the market."

Social media posts read, "The amount of people blaming and shaming Baily's Dairy makes me sad. Way too much judgment here." And "Can't imagine how stressful it has been for them." Another post read, "Only person that deserves blame here is the little idiot that escaped!"

Cavalcante was free of the police perimeter. For some hours, police didn't know that the murderer had eluded them and wasn't anywhere near Longwood Gardens, where they were patrolling. Cavalcante headed to the Phoenixville area, where he had family, business acquaintances, and a sometimes supportive Brazilian community. He needed assistance to continue his flight to freedom.

Cavalcante, unnoticed, made his way to the Bonnie Brae Road home of Robson Conegero, whom the murderer knew from family connections. Previously, Cavalcante visited Conegero's home "two or three times," according to testimony Conegero gave during Cavalcante's preliminary hearing on escape charges. Conegero said the first meeting took place about "three or four" years before the Saturday night visit. "Cavalcante was an acquaintance, nothing more," Conegero said. Conegero was aware that Cavalcante had escaped from the prison.

Conegero wasn't home on Saturday night. He was enjoying what he termed a "goodbye meal" in a restaurant near his home, for some relatives about to return to Brazil after a visit. He was with his wife, brother, daughter, father, mother, and grandparents. Conegero made the statements as he testified through an interpreter.

As the meal was concluding, Conegero received an alert on his cell phone from his Ring doorbell camera. Someone was on his front porch, attempting to contact him. The time was about 10:00 p.m. He looked at the image of the man, but he didn't recognize the person. He showed his wife the video. Immediately, his wife showed signs of becoming ill. "She was frightened," Conegero testified.

Conegero's wife was convinced the man in the hooded sweatshirt on their front porch was the escaped murderer. "I was still in doubt," Conegero testified.

After calming his wife, Conegero alerted police to the possibility that Cavalcante was on their property. Police officers responded to the scene and requested that Conegero immediately return home and detain Cavalcante as best he could until they arrived. Conegero feared for the safety of his family and delayed his departure until he was sure the police had arrived at his home.

The person on the porch who was believed to be the murderer was no longer in the area of Conegero's home. The tape from the Ring video was turned over to police. District Attorney Ryan said an FBI agent matched the voice on the video to Cavalcante. The video contained a key piece of information. The man in the hooded sweatshirt was seen with a vehicle key, and he was playing with the key by flicking the key in and out of its holder.

Cavalcante had access to a vehicle.

After failing to contact Conegero, Cavalcante headed to another person he knew in the community, Daniella Tunes, and her husband. They lived in the Eland Downe development just outside Phoenixville on Route 113.

Tunes recognized Cavalcante on her porch and wouldn't answer her doorbell. The time was about 10:30 p.m. She went to the second floor of her home and looked out a window and saw Cavalcante on the sidewalk near a white van, she recalled while testifying at Cavalcante's escape preliminary hearing. "I didn't allow him inside my home," she testified with the use of an interpreter. "I knew he had escaped."

Tunes testified that she was friends with Cavalcante's sister, and her husband worked with Cavalcante's brother-in-law. Tunes said she didn't speak with Cavalcante that evening.

Unsure of what to do, Tunes called a friend, and she urged the friend to contact police since she wasn't fluent in English. Police arrived within three minutes of being alerted by her friend. Tunes told police she was upstairs in her house when she saw a van departing. She couldn't see who was driving and couldn't see Cavalcante on the sidewalk or street.

Pennsylvania State Police reported receiving the call from Tune's friend just after midnight on September 10.

Now, the police knew through the Ring video and information from Tunes that Cavalcante had escaped the perimeter and was most likely driving a white van, even though he wasn't seen operating the vehicle. Police also knew that Cavalcante had changed his appearance. He was clean shaven. The change in appearance caused police to believe that Cavalcante was receiving assistance. At that point, law enforcement wasn't aware of all the material, including a Gillette razor, taken from the Drummond home.

A press release from the Pennsylvania State Police at 5:31 a.m. on September 10 stated, "On 09/09/23 during the late evening hours / overnight hours, it was reported that Danelo Cavalcante was seen in the northern Chester County area near Phoenixville. He changed his appearance. He is clean shaven and last seen wearing a yellow or green hooded sweatshirt, black baseball[-]style hat, green prison pants, and white shoes. He is operating an unknown vehicle possibly white in color." An update was later issued: "It is confirmed that Danelo Cavalcante is operating a 2020 White Ford Transit [van] bearing Pennsylvania registration ZST8818. The van has a refrigeration unit on the top. The vehicle is reported stolen by Baily's Dairy. Law Enforcement agencies nationwide have been advised."

FBI's Milligan received a call from Bivens in the early morning, reporting the escape of Cavalcante from the perimeter. "We were planning for another big shoulder-to-shoulder push at Longwood on Sunday," Milligan said. "I had assets coming in from other offices. The folks in our office were fantastic. We had other federal law enforcement partners reaching out to us to assist. The immigration office sent us thirty people to work the perimeter. The State Game Lands department pitched in. Once we knew he was out of the perimeter, we either shut down their approval or repurposed them for surveillance [of people Cavalcante knew in the Phoenixville area]."

Presently, the new video with Cavalcante's altered appearance was released to the public. The Pocopson community around Longwood Gardens breathed a sigh of relief. The fear was transferred to the populace surrounding Phoenixville, and especially the family of Cavalcante's murder victim. Sarah Brandao told reporters she was afraid that Cavalcante would come after her and her sister's two children, Yan and Yasmin. CNN reported Sarah Brandao saying, "I haven't slept for many days. I have been waking up with fright at night."

A frenzy of police activity took place in the early morning hours of Sunday, September 10, as soon as investigators realized that Cavalcante was no longer where they believed he was hiding.

The notice was received about three hours after Cavalcante's flight in the stolen truck. In that amount of time, Cavalcante could have been in any of three other states, if he had decided to drive away from Chester County.

Clark said he received a call in the middle of the night that Cavalcante had escaped the perimeter. Police believed Cavalcante was looking for an associate who previously resided in one of the houses, according to Clark. Clark alerted US marshal Eckman at 2:30 a.m. Eckman cut short his rest and headed from his home north of Phoenixville back to the command post at Po-Mar-Lin Fire Company.

"When I left my house, I saw one of our planes orbiting," Eckman said. "It was a clear night." Eckman arrived at the command post at 3:30 a.m. to find Clark there with members of the Pennsylvania State Police and Chester County detectives. "I remarked that this was really a good break for us," Eckman said. "I couldn't tell you what rock he was under in the woods. Now, I had information I could work with."

Clark added, "It was all about finding the vehicle. We found it quickly. We had made plans on what to do if he breached the perimeter." If Cavalcante had fled a great distance, police intended to fold their tents like a traveling circus and set up camp at the next sighting. Phoenixville was a quick drive from Pocopson. No folding of tents was required. The command post remained at the Po-Mar-Lin Fire Department.

To identify the vehicle, police—including Lt. Michael Stoner of the Embreeville barracks of the state police—began checking equipment that noted the license plates of cars driving between Longwood Gardens and Phoenixville. Vehicles viewed taking the route were deemed possible getaway cars.

Automated license plate readers are high-speed, computer-controlled camera systems that are typically mounted on street poles, streetlights, highway overpasses, or mobile trailers or attached to police squad cars. The readers automatically capture all license plate numbers that come into view, along with the location, date, and time. The data, which includes photographs of the vehicle and sometimes its driver and passengers, is then uploaded to a central server.

The van was identified through Chester County's automated readers. From the van's plate, the vehicle was traced to Baily's Dairy. Trooper John Pisker arrived at the Baily farm at 5:10 a.m. and informed Parsons of the theft. She didn't realize the van was missing.

"We calculated a possible route," Eckman said. Eckman reviewed the information and had a hunch as to where the van might be located. "We [US Marshal Service] had guys coming in about 6:00 a.m. I sent a photo and the area where we should search. We found the van in about twenty minutes. Not one person or agency recovered the van; we all worked together and applied the information we gathered."

The van was partially hidden off the road behind a barn in East Nantmeal Township, Chester County. Clark dispelled one of the rumors of the day. The van didn't run out of gas. Cavalcante was back in familiar territory and abandoned the van. The murderer was aware that at some point the stolen van would be traced to him.

A Pennsylvania State Police search team cleared the house and barn where the van was found. Rich DeRafalo owns an apartment house next to where the van was abandoned. When he arrived at his property, a number of non-law-enforcement people had gathered and sought permission to search the apartment house, especially an unoccupied unit, and his workspace to see if Cavalcante was secreting himself on the property.

"People were everywhere," DeRafalo said. "I gave them permission to search. Better they find him than me. I wasn't physically afraid of Cavalcante; I'm a big guy. But that changed when he became armed. Some of the people, in their thirties, were there looking to receive the reward money. They had their kids with them, I didn't understand that."

DeRafalo said his property wasn't his own for several days. Fox News and Channel 6 ABC television vans were in his driveway. US marshals were present. Roadblocks and police in riot gear with assault weapons changed his "awesome community," according to DeRafalo.

Cavalcante might have stopped in DeRafalo's garden for a tomato. "I can't say for sure, but I have a 30-by-40-foot garden, and I know what is in there. One was missing."

"The question before us," Clark said, "was did Cavalcante get picked up and leave the scene or was he still in the vicinity."

Cavalcante was smart enough not to directly contact his family. He told police he believed they would be under surveillance. The murderer was correct. The family was monitored from the time that Cavalcante's escape was known. Law enforcement was hoping Cavalcante would expose himself during a visit.

Once Cavalcante broke the perimeter, police knew that his sister Eleni Cavalcante had to be taken off the streets. She could provide her brother with resources to aid his escape. Eleni had visa issues with immigration authorities and was placed in custody, but she was later released. Another reason she was taken into custody was that Eleni had not been entirely truthful with police when questioned. At one point, she said she didn't know that her brother had escaped Chester County Prison, when indeed she did.

"The night Cavalcante stole the van," Eckman said, "we all agreed she had to go [placed in custody]. The request was quickly approved." Clark added, "We were concerned he would reach out to his sister. The sister was less than truthful in what she told us. That is why she was incarcerated. If she was more forthcoming to detectives, then she might not have been put in prison. We needed her out of the equation. One less resource was then available [for Cavalcante]."

Clark said he interviewed Eleni Cavalcante and her boyfriend, sometimes referred to as her husband, the day before her brother broke the perimeter. "She was upset, not arrogant or cocky," Clark said. "She answered my questions. She didn't have much to offer. I had a cordial conversation with her and her boyfriend."

A concern among law enforcement was that Cavalcante would flee back to his native Brazil. The United States doesn't have an extradition agreement with Brazil, and a possibility existed that Cavalcante would not be returned to serve his life sentence. Even if convicted of the Brazilian murder charge, Cavalcante would likely serve a shorter sentence in Brazil than in Pennsylvania.

As with the search surrounding Chester County Prison, law enforcement sought proof-of-life sightings. Known associates were tracked down and questioned. One person who assisted Cavalcante with the county murder was thoroughly interviewed, according to Eckman.

By midmorning on Sunday, word was spreading that the killer was on the loose in the northern section of Chester County. The populace began experiencing the same fears, stresses, and difficulties as those residing near the county prison. Schools were closed. One school had scheduled picture day for students, and it was canceled. Roadblocks were established and searches made.

Community members told reporters in the following days:

Today I can't get to work; I can't go down [Route] 23 because they have that shut down at [Route] 100. I tried to go across [Routes] 113 or 401. So, this is getting tough.

I can't even get from my house in Elverson to Phoenixville.

I can't take my kids to school right now. Everything's closed and I just got done talking to the school district in Boyertown and they're saying that it's probably safe to just take my kids back home and stuff for right now.

I had to go all the way around, and truthfully, I never seen so many state police at once, so it's very unsettling and very uncomfortable. I really hope that today is the day they finally catch him.

I don't want to bring a kid back into this area like this," one expectant mother said, fearing that Cavalcante might not be caught before she gave birth.

I would just love to see all of this come to a close.

Early Sunday morning, Ernie Hollings, chair of the nonprofit Mill at Anselma, had a decision to make. As with the Mushroom Festival, he had a public event scheduled that day. The mill is located close to where the van was discovered. A historical lecture on Lafayette was to be given at 3:00 p.m. by author Bruce Mowday. Previously, a Mowday lecture at the Crosslands community near the prison was postponed because of the Cavalcante search. Mowday was consulted. A decision was made to go forward with the lecture. The convicted murderer passed up the opportunity to learn about an American hero, Lafayette.

CHAPTER 12

END GAME

As Cavalcante switched locations, police prepared for a "long game," US marshal Clark told the media on Monday. The conclusion of Clark's long game was Cavalcante's capture. In the coming days, as a new batch of citizens fought off fear and thoughts of terror, police struggled to find the "proof of life" sightings that they desperately sought. Making tracking the murderer more difficult was a spate of false sightings.

To elicit additional help from the public, authorities upped the reward for information on Cavalcante's whereabouts from $20,000 to $25,000. The extra payoff might have sparked the increase in false reports.

A Phoenixville-area policeman reported that his office received a number of purported sightings, and many were of Hispanic men. A worry in the Hispanic community was that one of the bounty hunters would fire at an innocent Hispanic person in an effort to collect the reward.

Jeff Kimes, West Brandywine Township police chief, issued a social media warning to township residents on September 11. He wrote, "First, I would like to address social media during these high[-]profile events. Social media is a blessing (and a curse) when trying to push out timely and accurate information. Social media is a great tool for the PD to push out information, to our community, in a timely, efficient, and accurate way. The PD takes this role seriously, as we do not want to be a part of the rumor, personal individual thoughts, hearsay, false narrative, armchair quarterbacking, and inaccurate information platform. When any of these are projected into high[-]profile events, it adds to anxiety, stress, fear, and vulnerability. This is not something the PD wants to contribute and participate in an already highly tense situation. Unfortunately, there are times when NO information is better than false information. Neither circumstance is ideal, but when tasked with either, inaccurate/false information is not acceptable in my view."

Kimes's notification gave an update on the Cavalcante search. He wrote:

On September 10, the escaped individual made it to neighboring East Nantmeal Township, which is way too close for comfort for all of us. When it was discovered that the van he was driving was found abandoned in Nantmeal Village, our PD concentrated our patrols in Wallace. It's important to note that during this time, we received no credible information that this individual crossed into Wallace Township, nor was any information forwarded to us by the command post indicating such. We took it upon ourselves to concentrate our patrols in the northern end of Wallace for diligence. As of this writing (9/11/23), we still have not received any word that Wallace Township has been affected by this manhunt.

I want to make this clear, this has been a very trying time for residents and law enforcement in trying to capture this individual and return some normalcy and securement to our lives. As the tactics in trying to apprehend this individual are left to PSP to handle, I can say the multiple Law Enforcement agencies have been working around the clock, following up on leads and working in the scorching sun to drenching downpours, to bring this individual back to prison. This is a prime example of the community needing the PDs support, as the PD needing the community support, in working together, as one, for the common good of our society.

The PD wants all of our residents to feel safe and secure in their own homes. We are here to help facilitate the best we can. If you see anything suspicious or out of the norm, please call; we don't want anyone feeling insecure in their own home. We have increased patrols and are only a 911 phone call away. Thank you for your continued support in this partnership.

Law enforcement was worried about the murderer escaping the country, not into Wallace Township. Cavalcante was placed on Interpol's Red Notice. A red notice alerts police worldwide to internationally wanted fugitives. Marshal Eckman worked with Chester County detectives and District Attorney Ryan on the request for the Interpol notice. Eckman said in most cases, such a request takes several weeks to be approved. For Cavalcante, the notice was fast-tracked and approved within forty-eight hours of the request.

Possible sightings of Cavalcante took place Monday evening. The first tip came from a man who believed the escaped murderer was walking along Fairview Road. When police investigated, they found a set of footprints but not from prison-issued shoes. US marshal Clark said they had a photograph of the tread of a jail-issued shoe to compare tracks.

The search took them to the home of Jim Varnes.

Varnes and his wife had their television viewing interrupted. Varnes relayed his experience that night to a reporter. "We had people, cops in the driveway with flashlights and stuff. Then we saw SWAT teams there. It was a little frightening." The realization that Cavalcante was probably lurking outside their home, as close as 20 feet from where the couple was watching television, was indeed a shock.

Police discovered a pair of shoes on the property. A sweatshirt was also discarded. The footwear was believed to have been those of Cavalcante. Cavalcante had traded his prison-issued shoes for a pair of boots belonging to Varnes. "We walked out on the back porch. My wife did actually; she's the one that found my boots were missing," Varnes said.

Law enforcement officers and aerial support blanketed the neighborhood for hours. The manhunt put Varnes and his neighbors on edge. Some were in disbelief that the escaped murderer had transported himself to their community. One commented, "It's touch and go. You wake up in the middle of the night thinking, 'Why'd I wake up.' It's anxiety, you know?"

Another neighbor, South Coventry Township resident Horace Hammond of the 3500 block of Coventryville Road, had a closer encounter with Cavalcante.

Since the murderer was reported in his section of Chester County, Hammond carried a loaded .25-caliber Taurus pistol with him. He had the weapon while working in his garage on a welding project for a friend. A cautious and prepared man, Hammond wanted to ensure the safety of his partner, who usually returned from a work shift about 11:45 p.m. Hammond took his loaded "varmint rifle," a .22-caliber Ruger, that evening and lashed a flashlight to the barrel. He placed the weapon near the end of his workbench, propped against a wall. Hammond intended on taking it into the house with him when he finished working in the garage.

Cavalcante had other plans for the "varmint rifle." About 10:00 p.m. through an open garage door, Cavalcante spied the rifle and made a dash to retrieve the weapon before Hammond could react. Hammond believed he was about 12 feet away from Cavalcante when he first saw the escaped murderer. Hammond told the police he was seated and talking on the phone. Hammond couldn't prevent Cavalcante from obtaining the weapon and fleeing the garage.

"I told him, 'Don't do it, don't do it,'" Hammond testified at Cavalcante's preliminary hearing on escape charges. "And then I went after him."

The chase was on between the armed killer, the Ruger had ten rounds, and the armed homeowner with a small-caliber pistol. Clutching the rifle, Cavalcante ran through an opening between Hammond's garage and home and went eastbound toward a fence near a wooded area. Hammond testified that some words were exchanged with Cavalcante, but he couldn't recall the conversation. As Cavalcante ran up the hill northeast of the victim's home, Hammond fired four shots from his pistol. The shots missed the murderer.

"I thought I hit him," Hammond said. "Obviously I didn't."

A 911 call from Hammond immediately brought law enforcement to the scene. There was no doubt about a proof-of-life sighting this time. Police knew exactly where Cavalcante was located at 10:00 p.m. on Monday, September 11. To alert all law enforcement officers in the area that Cavalcante was armed, the state police decrypted radio broadcasts.

Trooper Aaron Botts of the Embreeville barracks of the state police interviewed Hammond. Botts reported that Hammond told him Cavalcante was shirtless. A search of the property revealed a discarded shirt and neon-green hooded sweatshirt. The sweatshirt matched the one Cavalcante was wearing in the video at the two Phoenixville-area residences.

At the command post, Clark said, the pieces of information were "all adding up. The shoes were taken not far from the shed where he took the rifle. We found his sweatshirt after he had fled the barn." There was a "high probability" that Cavalcante was losing his race for freedom.

US marshal Eckman responded to a call for a five-man team at the Hammond home. He recounted the chase. "We were told the team was needed to follow a tracking dog. They had Cavalcante's sweatshirt. They were using the shirt to give the dog a scent of Cavalcante. The dog smelled the sweatshirt and then we were off. We went up and down hills. We tracked him for an hour plus. We're not young; most of us were in our forties and fifties. One of us had bad knees. I have a messed-up back from a work-related injury. All I heard from our team were [groans]. The dog went off in the direction where Cavalcante fled, but lost him."

Despite the dogs losing the murderer's scent, the police perimeter was tightening around Cavalcante.

The Hammond encounter changed the investigation for the police and the public. Police now faced an armed murderer in Cavalcante. Police urged residents in the area of South Coventry Township to lock all doors, windows, and vehicles, and to shelter in place. Not only was the public at risk, but also law enforcement.

"When Cavalcante obtained the weapon, everything changed," Clark said. "We believed there was no way he was coming back alive. Some force, deadly force, was going to be used. He was armed. There was no way this was going to end well." Bivens told reporters that Cavalcante was always dangerous, and now he was "armed and extremely dangerous. He's killed two people previously. I would suspect that he's desperate enough to use that weapon."

Even Cavalcante's mother, Iracema, was doubting her son could survive. "I know what my son did was wrong," she told a Brazilian news reporter. "I know my son should pay for his mistake. But I want my son to pay for his mistake with dignity. Not to pay with his life." She commented to the *New York Times*, "Today, I see my son as dead. In a strange place, trampled, everyone lying about him, saying he's something he's not."

A component of police briefings was the use of force and what was appropriate when Cavalcante would be apprehended, according to Dr. Schiffer. "One of the things we discussed was if it was better for the system to have him dead or alive. It was better if he lived. If he would have been killed, then if another person escaped, that escapee would expect to die [and thus be more dangerous]. If taken alive, the message is we'll get you and you will be worse off [in prison]."

Tuesday morning, law enforcement concentrated on making sure Cavalcante didn't escape the perimeter again. Heavily traveled highways were closely monitored. Residents had a horrendous time commuting. Movement was also impossible for Cavalcante. He wasn't sighted that day. Schools in the Owen J. Roberts School District were closed for the second straight day. North Coventry Township police asked residents to stay away from the search areas. The defined perimeter included Routes 23 and 100, Fairview and Nantmeal Roads, and Iron Bridge and County Park Roads.

For Allison Jacobs and her daughter Kyndal, they didn't feel immediately threatened when news of Cavalcante's escape reached their Chester Springs home. Chester County had less crime than most places, especially large cities these days. "You hear all of the time about escapes and crime," Kyndal said. "It's different when you know the area where the crimes are taking place."

During the early part of the search, Allison and Kyndal visited Kennett Square to drop off some documents. Every road was closed, the mother and daughter recalled. Police and helicopters were everywhere. The lockbox for the documents was removed from the front of the building. The company didn't want to chance Cavalcante opening the secure box.

"It was both exciting and terrifying," Allison said. Soon after, Kyndal flew to a bachelorette party in Fort Lauderdale, Florida. "I sat next to a law enforcement officer who was involved with the search. Everyone in the airport was talking about Cavalcante. We couldn't wait to depart." The news followed Kyndal on her travels. A friend in Australia heard about the escape and contacted her.

When Cavalcante obtained the weapon, it became "more freaky," Kyndal said. Allison added, "Before I didn't lock my car; now I do." Allison is uncomfortable around weapons, but her son said he would obtain one for her. She added that many people in her community are hunters and have weapons.

The search area had many similarities to the area around Longwood. Bivens commented, "The search area is probably close to 3 miles across east to west and 2 to 2½ miles north to south. It's a large area of wooded, hilly terrain." Area residents were asked to make sure that cars and homes were locked and secure. Also, they were asked to review home security cameras and report to police any sightings of Cavalcante.

Constable Carozzo believed that the terrain in northern Chester County was more favorable to the searches than the Pocopson area. "The woods weren't as dense," Carozzo said.

One of the police investigators added, "All of the SWAT teams and FBI and border patrol teams did searches. The brush was so thick in certain areas that you had to get on your hands and knees to crawl through the thorns. We weren't prepared. We had clippers and machetes to hack away the undergrowth, but it was still too thick. It was too strong to get through."

The policeman added that they didn't know where they were going, and they would lose contact with the person next to them. "You gravitate to the path of least resistance, and we'd all end up together. There weren't even deer paths in some of the areas. The heat didn't help. There were no sightings that day. Some of the search teams went home midday."

Owen J. Roberts school superintendent Will Stout announced the closing of the schools under his direction. He added, "Our school sites are currently being used to support law enforcement initiatives, and we also recognize that many of our families have been under a tremendous amount of stress these past two days."

One area business owner, Bryan Donovan of the Horse Shoe Ranch in Pottstown, told the *Philadelphia Inquirer* in a phone interview he hadn't slept for more than forty-five minutes at a time since Cavalcante was reported in his community. The 500 acres that Donovan managed was in the middle of the search area. The hunt was causing havoc with his business. He noted that the helicopters circling about were stressing him, his employees, and his chickens. The company supplied eggs to a number of restaurants and grocery stores in the area. A driver on Donovan's Lancaster route didn't feel comfortable driving into the area. Multiple clients had their egg orders delayed for days.

Donovan added, "It's weird being out there wondering, 'Is someone in the woods watching me?' Am I going to drive past them on our farm?" Donovan additionally told the *Inquirer* reporter, "And there's a lot of vigilante people out there that shouldn't be out there that are driving around with guns, so then you're freaked out about them."

Looking out his window, Donovan reported seeing law enforcement combing through his field. Donovan abruptly but politely concluded the telephone interview with the reporter.

A number of businesses were affected by the manhunt, including the shops in Ludwig's Corner. Few customers visited the stores since a police barricade limited the traffic to the center, and citizens decided to stay home and not take the chance of encountering an armed escaped murderer. Many employees reported being on edge during the search. One business, Collective Coffee & Bakery, closed for the day at 11:00 a.m.

The employees weren't the only ones on edge in Ludwig's Corner. "There's homes nearby, schools, libraries, children," one employee told a reporter. "It makes it extremely terrifying for a lot of people."

The police search continued all day and evening without locating Cavalcante. Pennsylvania governor Josh Shapiro remained confident that police would capture Cavalcante. Shapiro issued a statement stating, "We have hundreds of law enforcement engaged in these communities, doing everything they can to both apprehend the suspect and keep people safe. I think they've responded well to each and every piece of information they've received, and I'm confident we're going to get this guy."

Shapiro announced that the state Department of Corrections would conduct a review of Cavalcante's escape from Chester County Prison, as well as two other recent escapes in Philadelphia and Warren County. "I have confidence in our state system, but we want to make sure that we shore up both our state and our county systems all across Pennsylvania."

The governor added that no evidence existed that Cavalcante received help while evading police. The governor issued a warning to anyone considering assisting the convicted murderer. Shapiro reminded the public that Cavalcante was now armed with a rifle. "If you do anything, anything to try and assist this individual, we will hold you accountable and prosecute you to the fullest extent of the law," Shapiro said.

Shapiro also had some advice for Cavalcante. He said, "As for the individual himself, this is a moment where you've got to realize the gig is almost up and you'd be best to turn yourself in."

The gig was almost up, as Shapiro indicated, but Cavalcante wasn't heeding Shapiro's advice. He wasn't about to surrender.

A false alarm brought police to a home on Prizer Road, South Coventry Township, about midnight. A homeowner went outside to smoke a cigarette, and he unintentionally set off his own burglar alarm system. Police responded in force. Bivens said that tactical teams had been searching an area not far from the home that night. "We did not find Cavalcante there, or anyone else, but it started to bring some of our people into that area," Bivens said.

The persistent surveillance finally brought results. At about 1:00 a.m. on Wednesday, September 13, a Drug Enforcement Agency plane equipped with thermal-imaging technology spotted a person in a section of woods in South Coventry Township. The person was believed to be Cavalcante. The image clearly defined a person, not a deer or other animal. The sighting was in a wooded area north of Prizer Road near Route 100, not far from Little's John Deere store.

"We had planes from all different services. They all had the same technology," Clark said. "We were informed we had a predator drone coming. I'm not sure if the drone was military or coming from the immigration department. The drone never made it to the search."

The evening was cooler than previous days of the manhunt. After six straight days of temperatures being 90 degrees or more, the high temperatures dropped into the 80s from September 9 through September 12. On Wednesday, the high would be only 79 degrees, with a low of 63 degrees.

A storm was fast approaching after the DEA spotting. Fearing for the safety of the plane and its crew, the plane landed until the storm passed. The entire region was under a flash-flood watch from 2:00 a.m. until 5:00 p.m. on Wednesday. The storm wasn't going to interfere with the search. "We'll keep an eye on anticipated weather conditions," said state police spokesperson Lt. Adam Reed. "Our troopers are equipped with proper rain gear to continue the search."

Rains were expected to fall at a high rate of 1 to 2 inches an hour, the National Weather Service reported, and some storms could contain damaging wind gusts.

The FBI SWAT team from Newark was on duty. Milligan said, "My overnight supervisor [at the command post] called that morning and told me they thought they had sighted Cavalcante. I thought to myself, I had heard that before and told him to keep me posted."

The deployed tactical search team was not about to give Cavalcante another chance to escape the dragnet. Bivens said, "Tactical teams made a decision to secure that area, that smaller area, as best they could and hold it through the storm and until we could bring additional resources in and bring aircraft back overhead to ensure that we did not have an issue with an escape."

Despite the rain and bad weather, the team formed a ring around the murderer's suspected position. They silently waited.

At sunrise, the DEA plane was again airborne.

About 8:00 a.m. the search resumed. Cavalcante was surrounded and surprised when he was confronted by the dozen members of the search team, including Cpl. Clinton Wagner of the Pennsylvania State Police Emergency Reaction Team. "They were able to move in very quietly. They had the element of surprise," Bivens said. "Cavalcante did not realize he was surrounded until that had occurred." The stolen .22-caliber Ruger rifle was close to him. Not wanting to give up, Cavalcante disobeyed a command to surrender and attempted to crawl through the thick underbrush. Cavalcante could not escape the pursuit of four-year-old K-9 Yoda of the US Border Patrol.

Seeing that Cavalcante wasn't going to surrender, Yoda was released by his handler, and the specially trained Belgian Malinois bit the murderer's head and prevented Cavalcante from fleeing. Clark said Yoda first bit Cavalcante's scalp and then latched on to his thigh. "I think he was in pain at that point," Clark said. "He was probably in excruciating pain."

At a press conference at the command post at the Po-Mar-Lin Fire Company in Unionville, Bivens reported that Yoda caused minor injuries to Cavalcante's scalp during his capture. "K-9s play a very important role not only for tracking but also for, in a circumstance like this, safely capturing someone," said Bivens. "It's far better that we're able to release a patrol dog like this and have them subdue the individual than have to use lethal force."

A US Border Patrol spokesperson confirmed that a member of the border patrol's tactical unit, known as BORTAC, released Yoda after Cavalcante attempted to flee. Law enforcement dogs are trained to attack once, but not repeatedly, and will release on command.

Yoda is a member of a tactical unit from El Paso, Texas. The American Kennel Club calls the Belgian Malinois a "smart, confident, and versatile" breed that works hard and forms unbreakable bonds with humans. Smaller and lighter than German shepherds, Belgian Malinois are frequently sought by law enforcement agencies for K-9 operations. The breed has assisted handlers in a variety of scenarios, from US military operations in Afghanistan to the details of US Secret Service agents at the White House.

At 8:18 a.m. on Wednesday, September 13, the thirty-four-year-old Cavalcante was back in custody. Cavalcante's freedom lasted just minutes short of a full thirteen days on the run.

When the command post was alerted to Cavalcante's capture, Eckman was working with members of the Chester County detectives on a plan to trap him. A Cavalcante associate had agreed to assist, according to Eckman. Also, a geospatial expert from the US Marshals Service had arrived to lend expert advice. A voice, Eckman said, announced, "They just got him. It was anticlimactic in some ways."

Following his capture, Cavalcante was taken to the Pennsylvania State Police barracks in Avondale, where they interviewed him before transferring him to the State Correctional Institution Phoenix in nearby Montgomery County, Pennsylvania. His inmate number was reported that day to be QP8931.

Dr. Schiffer was with Cavalcante from the time he was arrested until he was delivered to the Avondale barracks. "He [Cavalcante] was respectful and appropriate and never aggressive. He was a person," Schiffer said. "He was matter of fact. I didn't see anyone aggressive towards him. It was obvious he hadn't bathed in a few weeks. He was provided a bath before being given new clothing. He was treated as a person. That goes a long way on both sides."

During the interview, Cavalcante reported that he sustained himself on watermelons from farm fields and drank water from streams and creeks. His daily routine included hiding during the day and moving at night. He utilized the deep underbrush to conceal himself. Several times, officers passed a few feet from his location. He was also aware of the tracking dogs on his trail. To not give them a whiff of his scent, he kept his feces hidden.

Cavalcante's destination, according to the captured murderer, was to escape to New York City and then make his way to Canada. He eventually wanted to return to his native Brazil. Cavalcante hadn't devised a specific plan to make his way to New York. He was considering stealing another vehicle.

During the interview he confirmed what police suspected. Cavalcante indicated he had no assistance during his escape.

Eckman commented, "He was always considered dangerous. Our response changed when he secured the rifle. When [he was] not armed, our response would have been different than when he was armed. He is lucky to be alive, but he has to spend his life in a Pennsylvania prison. He was asked if he planned on shooting cops. 'No, if I wanted to, I could have,' he said. His plan was to carjack someone the next day. He said he hadn't planned on shooting anyone. Can you believe him? I've been involved in hundreds of homicide arrests, and he was one of the few I considered maniacal. I don't think he would have had issues killing anyone."

Clark said Cavalcante told investigators that he knew he had to pay for what he did but didn't want to pay with his life.

Brazilian prosecutor Rafael Pinto Alamy told the Associated Press that Cavalcante's plan to return home made sense, since Cavalcante faced a lighter sentence in Brazil if convicted of murder than the sentence he faced in the United States. "I thought he wanted to escape to Brazil," Alamy said. "He would have to comply with the prison rules there, which are much more lenient."

A Brazilian conviction carried a sentence of a maximum of thirty years in prison. The country does not impose life sentences. Cavalcante could be released after about twelve years for good behavior, according to Alamy.

During the long days of the hunt, members of the search teams never lost faith. They believed they would find Cavalcante and bring his days of freedom to an end. Some members of the search team planned to visit the Creamery in Kennett Square to have a few beers and celebrate. The celebration didn't take place. After the two-week search quietly ended in the morning hours of Wednesday, September 13, 2023, everyone just wanted to go home.

CHAPTER 13

AFTERMATH

Their two-week ordeal in the boiling sun and Chester County undergrowth was finished. Hundreds and hundreds of law enforcement officers involved in the successful search of Cavalcante could rest easy and return to their normal duties.

"The people of Chester County will never forget," US marshal Clark commented. "I won't forget."

Those capturing Cavalcante did some prideful celebrating. Photographs were taken of about two dozen officers in full tactical gear parading and posing with a handcuffed Cavalcante moments after his capture. At one point the officers were gathered in a half circle around the murderer. Their prey was trapped and brought to the ground.

The triumphal photograph drew criticism in some quarters, but not many, as inappropriate. Bivens dismissed the reproach. Bivens said, "They're proud of their work. I'm not bothered at all by the fact that they took a photograph with him in custody."

A Wednesday afternoon press conference announcing the capture of the murderer included unusual participants. Politicians, not seen during daily updates on the progress of the search, didn't pass up the opportunity to secure publicity before the gathered cameras. The previous press briefings featured mostly Bivens, Clark, Ryan, Sassa, and county law enforcement members explaining the progress made on the search. The crowd taking part in the climactic press conference was described as including "media personalities, elected officials, and law enforcement officers."

District Attorney Ryan told those gathered, "Today is a great day here in Chester County. Our nightmare is finally over, and the good guys won. Our community can finally regain its normalcy and breathe a collective sigh of relief. One of the high points during this crisis, in addition to all the support we received from law enforcement and our first responders, was that the community rallied behind us. We received hundreds of tips on our tip line, and we followed up on them all. We had hundreds and hundreds of meals donated by Wawa, churches, local organizations, and kind members of the community. Kids wrote sweet cards of support. Every day, people stopped by just to say thank you."

Bivens commented that despite the challenges the team faced and the length of time it took to capture Cavalcante, the operation was "absolutely" a success. No one, not least the fugitive himself, was seriously injured, Bivens said. He continued, "Our preference is always to use other means than lethal force. No one in the community was harmed, and no law enforcement was seriously harmed. That's a big win."

Governor Shapiro grasped the opportunity to go before the cameras during an afternoon press conference. Shapiro's most memorable remark was made in reference to the Philadelphia Eagles football team. Cavalcante was wearing a stolen Eagles hoodie sweatshirt when he was captured. Shapiro quipped, "Folks, whoever had their Eagles hoodie stolen, if you could let us know, I'll do my best to get you one of those new kelly-green ones."

Despite all the drama surrounding the search and capture of Cavalcante, Philadelphia news outlets all made time for the Eagles reference. Earlier in the year, the Eagles had played in the Super Bowl, and the region was still agog over the team. Some members of the public criticized the emphasis on the Eagles, stating that the focus of all the remarks should have stayed on the family of Cavalcante's murder victim and the dedication of those conducting the successful search for Cavalcante.

There were plenty of individuals and organizations to congratulate. One roll of participating agencies listed, besides the local police departments, the US Border Patrol, the FBI, the US Marshals Service, the ATF, the Pennsylvania State Police, the Chester County District Attorney's Office, and municipal partners in Chester, Montgomery, Delaware, and Bucks Counties. Noted on the list were trained K-9 dogs. High-tech equipment mentioned included planes, helicopters, drones, and thermal-imaging technology. Certainly, Cavalcante was outresourced during the thirteen-day search.

On September 13, Chester County Emergency Services posted, "For the past 12 days, EMS agencies across the region have been providing support to our law enforcement partners in their manhunt for (Danilo) Cavalcante. We want to acknowledge those EMS agencies and the EMTs, AEMTs, and Paramedics involved in supporting this dangerous search. THANK YOU!" The listed agencies were Longwood Fire Company and its Primary EMS support, Tactical Paramedics, Minquas Fire Company No. 2 and its Tactical Paramedics, and Good Fellowship Ambulance and its Tactical Paramedics and Rehab Unit.

In Cavalcante's native Brazil, his capture merited front-page newspaper coverage. Relatives of the man whom Cavalcante was charged with murdering in Brazil told the paper *Folha de S. Paulo* that they were relieved that Cavalcante was captured and spending time in prison, even though in a foreign country.

"We're pleased [with his capture], but there was no justice for my brother in Brazil. Justice is very slow," said Dayane Moreira dos Reis, the victim's sister. "We [now] hope he'll stay in prison for his whole sentence."

The Chester County public, especially those residing near the prison in Pocopson Township, were thankful that the two-week ordeal had concluded. At the Pocopson

Township building, where the first press conference took place, Aledia Diaz, administrative assistant for the township, told a reporter, "We are really very relieved that he has been caught. We'd been locking our doors and windows and leaving on the exterior house lights at night." Diaz, who lives in Kennett Square, continued, "We locked all our car doors. I think that they did a great job in capturing him. They were up against a lot. I am grateful to them."

Longwood Gardens issued a statement thanking those aiding in the murderer's capture. "Longwood Gardens wishes to express our deepest gratitude to law enforcement, authorities, and government officials for their tireless work in apprehending Danelo Cavalcante. We are grateful for the peaceful conclusion and thank all those involved in the search for their unwavering dedication. We look forward to our community returning to normal activity and look forward to welcoming guests back to the serenity and beauty of our Gardens."

The general public was grateful. On Friday, September 29, 2023, more than two weeks after the capture, members of the US Marshals task force were part of a leadership-training tour. The location was the American Revolution's Brandywine Battlefield, near where the search for Cavalcante was conducted. The exercise was planned long before the escape. At a stop at an East Bradford Township park, just north of Lenape, a visitor learned that the marshals were on the bus. She made her way to the bus and at the front thanked them personally for their hard work and sacrifices and keeping her family and community safe. The unsolicited statements were greatly appreciated by the marshals. The woman was told that law enforcement greatly appreciated all the supplies donated by the community aiding in the search effort.

The public was overly generous throughout the search. Longwood Fire Company, at one point, asked the public to curtail contributions. A fire company social media posting read, "Thank you to all those residents looking for a way to assist the ongoing incident with the escaped prisoner. We are supporting our law enforcement partners in some logistical capacities, but we are NOT currently in need of any food, water, or other supplies. If we do seek these items in the future, we will communicate the request through all social media platforms with specific information for when and where to donate. For now, we just ask that you use caution in and around the affected area and stay safe. Thank you again to all of those looking to help."

Christine Griffith, secretary of the Po-Mar-Lin Fire Company, wrote an account of the company's experience as command headquarters. Chief Jason Griffith said the members "rode the same rollercoaster of emotions as the command center personnel." At first, Chief Griffith didn't believe the operation would last too long. As the days mounted, Griffith had to maintain protection of his coverage area while providing assistance for the search for Cavalcante.

Even with the cramped space, law enforcement was never intrusive and reinforced that the firehouse was the firefighters' house. Local residents dropped off supplies, from food, water, and bug spray for the investigators, to dog treats for the K-9s. Po-Mar-Lin members offered their expertise on the area and supplied maps. Fire company personnel were an integral part of the search.

A reader of the *New York Times* commented, "I'm glad Cavalcante was caught. His past history is unfortunate, even sad, but he is what he is, a murderer who stabbed a young woman multiple times, with her children present to see it happen. He not only killed his ex-girlfriend, he traumatized her children, who are now motherless and who will never be free of the memory of that horrible scene. There is no undoing what he did, and as he himself said, he must pay for it."

Some normalcy returned to the county. Businesses welcomed customers, visitors to Longwood Gardens strolled the beautiful landscape without fear of passing a murderer, and students returned to classrooms. Resident Jennie Brown told a reporter she didn't want to have to repeat her Labor Day experiences. "Many neighbors had a police officer on their deck with a machine gun while they slept," she said. "I've never felt more scared, and more safe at the same time. It's a really strange feeling."

While thankful for Cavalcante being behind bars, not everyone was satisfied. The populace demanded assurances from elected officials that another murderer, or any other criminal, wouldn't escape. They wanted answers to what went wrong to allow the murderer to roam the public. Not all the members of the public could go back to their normal lives. Some suffered from posttraumatic stress.

Ryan Drummond and his family remained traumatized by the murderer's invasion of their home long after Cavalcante's capture. "The paranoia is there," Drummond said. The homeowner and father said that every night he believed he heard a noise or saw a flash of light in his kitchen, just as when he encountered during Cavalcante's invasion of his home. Long after the murderer was back in custody, Drummond reported standing on the second floor of his home, baseball bat in hand, listening for any sign of an intruder.

Elected officials determined that a series of town meetings would be the best way to handle the onslaught of questions. Some of the inquiries were angry, some accusatory, and some political, since an election for county officials was just two months away.

Less than a week after Cavalcante was taken into custody, the first town meeting was held at Chadds Ford Elementary School on Monday, September 18. The school sat on one of the perimeters of the search. The scheduled meeting time was 7:00 p.m. Officials were expecting angry constituents. Signs were posted at the entrance, pleading with attendees to be respectful of others. A second town meeting took place at Owen J. Roberts Middle School, 881 Ridge Road, Pottstown, on Monday, October 2 at 7:00 p.m.

Greeting those attending the Chadds Ford meeting was a line of television cameras from Philadelphia and surrounding stations. Reporters, with microphones in hand, were soliciting comments from residents. The cameras were barred from filming the town meeting. Was the order to keep peace in the meeting? The cameras might entice some in the audience to act out inappropriately. Or was the order to make sure a video record of the town meeting wasn't available? One resident asked the county what they wanted to hide, and that the news media had every right to be present and "to listen to your BS."

The government reply was "We wanted this experience to be with residents, a personal setting. That's why media couldn't come. We wanted a face-to-face. Media was invited. They're outside." That answer wasn't accepted by many in the community.

Before the start time, all the parking spaces at the school were filled and vehicles were parking in fire lanes. The meeting was held in the school's gymnasium, with folding chairs separated into two groups in the middle of the floor. The two hundred chairs were about filled when the meeting commenced just a few minutes later than the announced starting time. A projector was used, but the lighting in the vast room made the images on the screen difficult to see. The sound system wasn't loud enough for all to hear. The video and audio deficiencies didn't help the restless mood of the audience.

Chester County commissioner Josh Maxwell, chair of the county's prison board, began the meeting. Notably absent were many members of the prison board. More than one spectator noted that the elected officials were more interested in getting reelected than doing their jobs, especially having to answer for the deficiencies of the prison system.

Maxwell began by saying the past seven days were a "historic week" for the county. He didn't elaborate if the history should be considered good or bad or if the whole incident should be classified as infamous. Clearly, the attendees were leaning toward the "infamous" label.

Chester County commissioner Marian Moskowitz acknowledged the "emotional impact on the community." The county had counselors ready to help citizens cope with the psychological turmoil.

The third Chester County commissioner, Michelle Kichline, connected with the citizens more than her colleagues. She apologized to them and said she was sorry for what the community had to endure. Kichline said at times she recognized fear in their faces. What the public encountered was unthinkable, Kichline said.

Kichline took a moment to correct one of the many erroneous statements posted on social media. Crimes committed by illegal aliens are condemned by a majority of the public, and sanctuary cities are blamed by many for protecting murderers and other vicious criminals. Kichline said that Chester County is not a designated sanctuary county, and the county does not interfere with federal officials apprehending such criminals.

The next person speaking was the man on the hot seat, acting warden Howard Holland. Holland's first official day on the job was the escape day. When he was first told of the potential absconder, Holland said he believed it was just a gag being played on him by his new staff. Then, Holland heard people running in the hallway. The alert was serious. Holland told the audience he was "shocked." The prison personnel launched into their escape procedures to try to locate Cavalcante. He was not in the prison.

Holland indicated the alarm siren was activated. The audience responded that they didn't hear the warning, and that the siren had been mistaken for a train whistle. Holland told the crowd that he and his staff were convinced Cavalcante was in the immediate area, and a command post was established at the prison. Emotions were running high at the prison, and the correctional officers were embarrassed, Holland said.

To protect the public in the future, Holland discussed some of his plans for enhanced security, including high-tech equipment, additional barbed wire, and additional correctional officers. The public, during their turn to question, asked Holland about his staff. Holland told the public that the employees were at 60 percent of being fully staffed. The public had another logical question for Holland. If the prison didn't have enough correctional officers to safely protect the public, why wasn't the number of prisoners, especially dangerous ones, reduced? Of course, the prison takes what prisoners the justice system sends them. The prison has no control on the inflow of inmates.

Holland volunteered that the clothing issued to prisoners would change. No longer would prisoners be allowed to dress in civilian clothes. Residents will readily be able to identify prisoners as inmates by their outfit. The public wondered why the clothing change had not taken place before the escape.

"I want them to know that we take responsibility for what happened here," Holland told the audience. "We take it seriously. Everybody was put in harm's way." Holland also acknowledged that the manhunt took away a sense of security for thousands of neighbors of the prison.

Also speaking before the group was the director of emergency services, Bill Messerschmidt. He explained the workings of the ReadyChesCo electronic notification system. Some members of the public in the audience indicated they weren't aware of the system, and others signaled they hadn't signed up for the notifications. Some who did complained that they never received alerts, the alerts were too limited in geography, the alerts were untimely, or the information in the alerts wasn't sufficient. Messerschmidt said the information and broadcasting area was controlled by the Pennsylvania State Police.

The town hall was opened for questions, and citizens lined a wall waiting for their turn to comment or question the gathered officials.

Some of the statements included the following:

> Why are dangerous criminals housed in Chester County Prison? I was told by the township years ago that only criminals charged with minor offenses, such as drunk driving and shoplifting, would be housed there.
>
> It was stressful taking care of my eighty-one-year-old mother in the township (during the escape).
>
> This is not why I came to live in Pocopson Township.
>
> Home values have declined.
>
> Who is going to pay? Businesses have lost money.
>
> Alerts should have gone to everyone in the county, not just a 6-mile radius.

Cavalcante could have reached my home within minutes, and I wasn't alerted until two and a half hours passed.

Please keep the community informed.

A man who worked at Longwood and lived with his family there, including small children, walked the family dog with a 9 mm pistol in one hand and a leash in the other.

I couldn't sleep. My wife couldn't sleep. We spent the night with a weapon, looking out the window at an adjoining field. We kept the screen off the window so we could have a better line of sight.

Terrifying!

The lack of information meant false information was being spread.

Why weren't there dogs at the prison?

Some of our taxes should be used to take care of the K-9s.

My wife couldn't walk down the hall for a glass of milk, she was so scared.

A woman who lived outside Chester County said she didn't feel safe, and she was getting a dog.

My kids couldn't sleep. My wife couldn't sleep. I was pacing my woods just listening in case someone walked through. Every night I was in my bathroom looking out the window with my 9 mm, listening to the woods all night long. The night he made it to Folly Hill I saw a flashlight in my woods, and I've never seen a flashlight in my woods. No information spreads false information. After Spider-Man went up the wall, would you be willing to hire a few carpenters to box the areas out until the measures are in place?

What happened to bright-orange pants? My wife said she thought an escaped prisoner was in our yard. I said it's gotta be a landscaper. We had to put it together to realize it was a prisoner. I didn't expect to be doing this investigative work as a resident. My wife and I were disgusted during the press conferences. Lots of fancy names for this wire—it's barbed wire. You say you didn't anticipate this happening, but it did, just months ago, so what now? This guy walked through my backyard, and my child waved at him like she does to everyone. That will haunt me forever. It's gross negligence. It didn't need to happen. If you sorted out the last one, we wouldn't be here.

The county held other town meetings and the Pocopson Township Supervisors meeting on September 24, 2023, to comment on the escape and to handle other township business.

The township meeting drew about fifty people, much fewer than the county's town meetings. There was plenty of parking, and only two television stations sent representatives. Supervisors Elaine DiMonte and Raymond McKay attended the meeting. Ricki Stumpo was absent because of a religious holiday. Item 16 on the agenda was "Remarks from County Officials Regarding Prison Escape—County Commissioner Josh Maxwell, Acting Warden Howard Holland, and Department of Emergency Services Director Bill Messerschmidt."

During this presentation, Maxwell acknowledged the "gravity" of the escape. The supervisor also commented that the prison board became concerned about the running of the prison the previous year and hired experts to study the prison's operations. Maxwell said complaints were made by staff as to working conditions. Maxwell said the prison board was concerned enough to hire Holland as their "eyes and ears."

"This prison needs a lot of work," Maxwell commented. The county planned to install new cameras and hire enough staff to have eight persons monitoring the cameras. The county was going to look into grant money to reinstate the K-9 unit.

Holland gave the audience some additional information. He said some razor wire was added after the Bolte escape. Obviously not enough was placed to deter Cavalcante. Holland said at that moment the prison had 301 authorized positions and sixty-nine vacancies. Pay had been increased 9 percent to help attract new employees. Going forward, the prison was going to concentrate on three areas, "security, technology, and operations."

As to deter future escapes, Holland said additional razor wire would be added, and the prison administration would focus on three issues. They are "Detection, Delay Escape, and Response." Holland did mention that additional razor wire had been authorized two weeks before Cavalcante's escape, but a lack of supplies delayed installation.

Communications among government, county and township, and citizens were heavily criticized, once again. A citizen declared, "The lack of communication during the search was appalling." Another resident said, "I'm having trust issues." She said she stopped using the township's exercise trail around the prison. Residents complained they received numerous warnings about sheltering in their homes but were never alerted when they could depart. Maxwell admitted, uttering an understatement, that "communication was subpar."

Holland indicated that he understood the trust issues and said he recommended changes after the Bolte escape, but his suggestions were ignored. As for the lack of information about the Bolte escape, Holland agreed with the resident's comment. The citizen said it would be better to "overwarn" residents than "underwarn" them. The community should have been told about the Bolte escape.

One resident wanted to know how Cavalcante knew about Bolte's prison escape, when the public wasn't informed. Holland said, "There are no secrets in jail. He was in the prison for weeks, and he knew of the prior escape."

As to the state of the prison, Holland commented, "I feel stuck in 1981." When asking his staff about seemingly outdated procedures, Holland said he was told "that is the way we have always done it."

One major change was the time needed to transfer prisoners to state prison after sentencing. Previously the prisoner was held for thirty days. This was the time period when Cavalcante escaped. There is no regulation mandating prisoners being held at county prisons before being transferred to state prisons. Now, the prison is working with the county's Clerk of Courts Office to speed up the paperwork for transfers.

The lack of trust included the county's prison board. Residents wanted representation on the board. The board's members are designated by the commonwealth and are limited to elected officials. A township liaison, with no voting power, is being considered being added to the prison board.

While most of the residents were skeptical of the responses and promises of the elected officials, one woman was reassured. She said she was afraid for the first time in her life during the escape. "I'm not afraid now," she declared. Another resident said she wasn't convinced a prison escape wouldn't take place in the future.

The wrath of the public wasn't confined to town hall meetings. Residents attended the Chester County Prison Board and commissioners' meetings. During those meetings, county officials promised upgrades, costly upgrades, to the prison.

At a prison board meeting, members approved purchasing fifty to seventy-five cameras to place around the prison perimeter, and eight new full-time security camera operators to monitor cameras. The board also agreed to provide additional security training for correctional officers and improve coordination with Pocopson Township.

Design upgrades to enhance security for exercise yards were fast-tracked with the awarding of a $94,000 contract to TranSystems, LLC, of Ebensburg, Cambria County. Brian Endler, vice president of engineering and an architect at TranSystems, promised a temporary system could be installed within six months.

Ebensburg has connections to the murderer Norman Johnston, who later roamed Chester County as an escapee. Johnston's murder trial was held in Ebensburg. During that two-month court proceeding, Chester County taxpayers paid for security updates at the Cambria County prison and courthouse.

The *Daily Local News* noted that "members of the Chester County Prison Board have agreed to upgrade the physical barriers to outdoor recreational yards at the Pocopson facility, enclosing them with walls and roofing that a consultant said would eliminate the building flaws that allowed two men—one a convicted murderer—to escape the prison this year."

The newspaper reporter described the action taken "as residents continued to vent their anger at the county officials whose perceived lax oversight of the prison allowed the escape of Danilo Cavalcante to happen. Residents said the escape left the county in fear, and said they were frustrated at the slow pace of capture, and afraid to leave their homes."

The meeting lasted two and a half hours as residents took turns being critical of the administration. "The board—the three county commissioners, the county district attorney, the sheriff, and the county controller—voted to proceed with the solution laid out by the TranSystems firm brought in by acting warden Howard Holland that would turn the recreation areas from outdoor open-air yards to indoor gymnasium-like rooms.

"The cost of the project, which a TranSystems representative said could begin this fall, was set at between $2.5 million and $3.5 million. It will be paid for out of American Rescue Plan Act funds left over from the pandemic."

While residents demanded and applauded the tough new measures, not everyone was cheering. The Pennsylvania Prison Society, an advocacy group for prisoners' rights, had concerns. The society especially didn't like the idea of enclosing the exercise yards with a solid roof.

"In their rush to reassure the community, county officials are pursuing expensive, misguided solutions that will degrade the physical and mental health of incarcerated people: they plan to completely enclose exercise yards with a solid roof, effectively depriving them access to fresh, open air and sunlight," said the group's release.

On September 20, the prison board approved the design concept that would convert all eight of the jail's outdoor exercise yards into indoor facilities. The designs indicate that an 18-foot outer wall of solid masonry will replace the current chain-link fence and a solid roof over the open sky. The only opening that would admit air and natural light from outside would be a narrow "ribbon" of windows running along the top of the wall.

The plan to upgrade the security at the prison came even as Holland has said that there had been only three escapes in the past twenty years—including two by the same man—and there had been no other significant security issues brought to the prison administration officials over the years.

EPILOGUE

The capture of Cavalcante after the most massive and costly manhunt in the history of Chester County didn't conclude the affair. For many in the community, the escape will have lingering residue for years.

The episode is not over for the justice system, since Cavalcante's trial on escape and other charges was pending in May 2024. The murder charge in Brazil against Cavalcante is awaiting adjudication.

The episode is not over for Chester County officials. The failures that led to the escape need to be rectified. The trust of the citizenry needs to be regained.

The community needs to deal with lingering uneasiness, from PTSD to the fear of another escape. For taxpayers, the bill for the escape is immense, estimated to be about $15 million for the search plus the hundreds of thousands of dollars more for fixes at the prison. The loss to businesses will add millions to the bill.

In time, Cavalcante's name will fade from the consciousness of most of the population. There will be notable exceptions: the families of the murderer's victims.

Two weeks after the capture, members of the Chester County Detectives Office and the US Marshals Service visited the Phoenixville home of Sarah Brandao and her niece and nephew, Yasmin and Yan Brandao. Detective David Nieves has been involved in the case since the murder of Deborah, Sarah's sister and the mother of Yasmin and Yan.

Nieves brought a special surprise for Yan: two signed pictures and a letter from Yoda's handler in Michigan. Yoda was the K-9 involved in the capture of Cavalcante. One of the photos was signed with Yoda's paw print. The other read, "Yan, may the Force be with you, always." The gifts made Yan "happy," according to sister Yasmin.

Community members haven't forgotten Deborah Brandao. One wrote on social media, "My thoughts, love, and light sent for healing to the victim's family, and reverent hope that Deborah Brandao is resting peacefully." The writer had a special message for Cavalcante: "Enjoy the next 50 years in prison, Dirt bag."

Unionville Times editor Mike McGann had his own message for county government. He lives about 500 yards from Chester County Prison. McGann wrote in a column:

> The truth is, though, there have been issues about the county complex going back decades—I've lived here almost 25 years.
>
> Decisions made more than a decade ago contributed to the escape—decisions driven by political leaders who could never bring themselves to raise taxes, even if it meant cutting corners and hoping for the best. Chester County doesn't pay particularly

well and continues to have staffing problems both for deputies and corrections officers. Ironically, the Cavalcante search will likely end up costing millions of dollars, but had the county spent a fraction of that on more staff for the prison over the last decade, the escape might never have happened.

Longwood Fire Company chief McCarthy agreed with McGann. McCarthy said Chester County, one of the wealthiest counties in the land, continuously underpays employees. "It baffles my mind where they spend money and where they don't."

Did Chester County learn any lessons from the Cavalcante escape? McCarthy is "disappointed" that his organization, the one supplying logistics for the search, hadn't been contacted about contributing to an after-action report. "I was told PSP was doing one," McCarthy said. "We were an entire division of this operation and haven't talked to anyone. It didn't go the way it should have."

Also unsettled, according to McCarthy, is reimbursement for services rendered. Longwood forwarded an invoice to the Pennsylvania State Police for $20,000 and it is unpaid, and McCarthy was told it wouldn't be paid. The invoice could have totaled $45,000, but the company "ate" part of the expenses, according to McCarthy. Also, company administrators, including McCarthy, didn't receive compensation. "I had to bring in extra people and pay overtime," McCarthy said. "I had trucks on standby, meaning they could help protect the community. I had equipment damage, including one of our Zodiacs [a water rescue boat[. One truck was utilized almost twenty-four hours a day to offer comfort for the investigators and the normal charge is $400 per hour.

"The state police said they weren't paying anyone's expenses. The county told me once Cavalcante left the prison, it wasn't their responsibility. This isn't fair to our community. Our taxpayers are left with paying the hefty costs. If this happens again, I told my board of directors we won't offer assistance until we are assured we will be paid. We'll protect the community, but someone will pay."

McCarthy added, "Think about Longwood Gardens. Thousands of people a day come to the gardens. Imagine what they lost. And the Karco owners, I'm amazed they are still in business. The total loss to the community has to be in the tens of millions of dollars. And there is no mechanism to recover costs for them."

Eight months after being named acting warden, Howard Holland had the "acting" designation taken from his name. Three persons were interviewed for the full-time warden's position before Holland was given the job. On April 29, 2024, Holland received the promotion by the prison board. Commenting on the appointment, chair of the prison board Maxwell said, "In the eight months that Howard Holland has served as acting warden, Chester County Prison has seen improvements in safety and security systems, with plans to continue strengthening security measures."

During the meeting where he was appointed warden, Holland commented, "We are enhancing [the training] we are giving to our personnel, giving them a better chance to be successful."

Holland has changed the prison's escape risk policy. The announced changes appear to be the same as the ones enforced prior to COVID. Now, the prison takes measures to prevent an escape from inside the prison as well as during prisoner transports. According to county government, "This includes assignment of different[-]color clothing indicating a potential escape risk, and monitoring by one correction officer to one inmate—or two corrections officers to one inmate—when outside the prison cell."

During town halls and meetings of the Chester County Prison Board and commissioners, many costly promises were made to upgrade the security at Chester County Prison.

In October, Holland reported that razor wire was installed around the entire perimeter of the prison. The "fifty to seventy-five" security cameras had not been installed, he said. The Chester County Prison Board awarded an $118,697 contract to Unlimited Technology Inc., Chester Springs, to install cameras on the roof and around the fence of the county jail.

Holland did report that prisoners are transferred to state prisons as soon as possible and not waiting thirty days as was the previous practice. And high-level inmates are wearing brightly colored prison uniforms.

Holland indicated that the roof areas will be closed off with metal fabrications. The prison board awarded a $94,000 contract to design security upgrades for exercise yards to TransSystems, LLC, Ebensburg, Cambria County.

The prison, according to Holland, is also looking at using K-9 dogs for security and closing the exterior. The prison was accepting applications for correction officers. The starting salary for an officer is $24.40 an hour.

Not all the changes were at the prison. In October 2023, the Chester County Court of Common Pleas president, Judge John Hall, issued an order making changes in the way inmates were transported, to "better ensure the functioning of court operations" and to "provide adequate safety" to those in the courthouse. The order was issued because of the significant shortage of deputy sheriffs.

The *Daily Local News* reported, "The new rules, some of which, such as armed personnel and transportation, are unprecedented in the history of the county courts. Hall said it would be up to the president judge, the sheriff, and the county court administration to determine when the new rules would be lifted."

In November 2023, the Pennsylvania attorney general filed twenty new charges against Cavalcante, including felony counts of burglary, criminal trespassing, theft, and possession of a firearm. Investigators allege that Cavalcante, who was serving a life sentence for murder, stole items to help him change his appearance, a getaway vehicle, and a rifle with ammunition.

According to the charges, Cavalcante burglarized two homes in Pennsbury and South Coventry Townships, stealing the firearm, clothing, and a shaving razor. He is also charged with stealing a Ford transit van from a location in Pocopson Township.

Plea negotiation discussions reportedly took place, calling for additional prison time for Cavalcante in exchange for a guilty plea. A deal was not made. A trial, meaning added expense for the taxpayers, was on the court docket as of May 2024.

On May 6, 2024, Cavalcante changed attorneys as Lonny Fish of Philadelphia took over Cavalcante's defense. Fish appeared before Chester County Court of Common Pleas judge Allison Bell Royer, who is presiding over Cavalcante's escape. The case was continued to the June 26, 2024, criminal term.

The year 2023 was dubbed the year of escape by a number of publications in the Chester County and Philadelphia areas.

One publication reported, "The eyes of the region, the nation, and indeed, the world turned towards Chester County in the late summer of 2023, and not for the grandest of reasons. For two weeks in August and September, the name of a short, curly-haired, Brazil native seemed to be on the lips of everyone in the media and the local population: Danilo Cavalcante. The 34-year-old laborer who lived in Montgomery County before his arrest on first-degree murder charges in 2021 had escaped from Chester County Prison after being convicted at trial and brought fear, frustration, and a bit of fascination to the county."

The local Patch internet news outlet's named top-read articles of the year were about Cavalcante. "The escape of convicted killer Danilo Cavalcante put Chester County in the national spotlight, leaving residents living in fear, and causing law enforcement officials to work overtime, combing through brush and fields in northern Chester County." In December 2023, Patch reported that two other Pennsylvania prisoners, one in Philadelphia and one in Blair, were on the run after escapes.

One escaped prisoner from Missouri had a few extra days of freedom courtesy of the Cavalcante hunt. The US marshals were tracking Mario Che-Tiul when the department was dispatched to help corral Cavalcante. A week after Cavalcante was in custody, Marshals arrested Che-Tiul in Avondale, not far from the state police barracks, and taken to Chester County Prison. Che-Tiul was charged with child sexual assault. He had escaped on June 1.

While the world watched the search for Cavalcante, another hunt in Washington, DC, received little attention, according to one national newspaper. Christopher Haynes, charged with murder, escaped from George Washington University Hospital on September 6. A news article reported, "The contrast between the two manhunts has been stark: while the national media has tracked every development in Cavalcante's flight, Haynes has basically dropped off the map. Police were able to provide an image last week of Haynes wearing a black T-shirt and gray briefs and moving through a local backyard. But the only updates since then have been the offering of a $25,000 reward for information leading to his capture and a news release increasing the reward to $30,000 and providing additional details about the escape.

"Brian Levin, criminal justice professor emeritus at California State University San Bernardino, believes the difference in public attention and media coverage comes down to a number of factors. For starters, there's the viral video of Cavalcante's innovative escape from Chester County Prison as he braced himself between two walls and performed a sort of vertical crab-walk up and out of sight. 'There were all these aspects that were Hollywood-esque,' Levin said. 'The video of that crab-walk up the wall looked like something out of a movie.'"

US Marshals recaptured Haynes on October 26 in Maryland.

Chester County wasn't the only commonwealth county having escape issues. Philadelphia's KYW news outlets reported that the big city had three known escapes from Philadelphia jails in 2023.

And some healing was taking place in the community. Parsons, one of the owners of Baily's Dairy, where an escape van was stolen, said she was invited to a Halloween party in October 2023 in the Waterglen community, where Cavalcante terrorized the residents. "We came with the van and we brought ice cream, candy, and chocolate milk," Parsons said. "It was a healing process for us and Waterglen. It was cool. Everyone had their own stories to tell."

By Halloween, some saw humor in the Cavalcante saga as adults wore Cavalcante costumes to Halloween parties. Not all found Cavalcante amusing, since one student at Unionville tried to do so for a party and "got in trouble."

Cavalcante and Johnston were never a jest to the community; they caused fear, anxiety, PTSD, financial setbacks, and a sense of loss of safety in their neighborhoods.

APPENDIXES

APPENDIX A: TIMELINE

July 3, 1989	Danilo Souza Cavalcante is born in Estreito, Maranhão, Brazil.
November 5, 2017	Valter Júnior Moreira dos Reis is shot to death in front of a restaurant in Figueiropolis, Tocantins, Brazil. Brazilian authorities name Cavalcante as a suspect in Reis's death.
January 2018	Cavalcante flies to Puerto Rico and then enters the United States through New York Harbor and settles in Chester County, where his sister lived.
June 2018	Cavalcante is named as a fugitive in Brazil's national warrant information system.
June 2020	Cavalcante is charged with assaulting his girlfriend Deborah Brandao.
April 18, 2021	Cavalcante murders his ex-girlfriend Deborah Brandao by stabbing her thirty-seven times in front of her children at the victim's Schuylkill Township home.
April 19, 2021	Cavalcante is arrested by Virginia State Police in Prince William County, Virginia.
February 2023	Chester County commissions a $28,985 study by the National Institute for Jail Operations for training and a "comprehensive evaluation" to review policies and procedures, and overall working conditions at the prison.
April 2023	Downingtown police chief Howard Holland is hired by Chester County as a special liaison to the prison.
May 19, 2023	An escape takes place from Chester County Prison by inmate Igor Bolte.

July 2023	National Institute for Jail Operations renders a report on Chester County Prison conditions.
July 2023	Prison correctional officer alerts superiors that Cavalcante is planning an escape.
July 28, 2023	Warden Phillips is placed on administrative leave.
August 16, 2023	Cavalcante is convicted of first-degree murder in the death of Deborah Brandao by a jury after fifteen minutes of deliberations.
August 22, 2023	Cavalcante is sentenced to life in prison by Judge Patrick Carmody.
August 31, 2023	Holland's first day as acting warden. 8:33 a.m. Cavalcante enters exercise yard. 8:51 a.m. Cavalcante begins crab-walking up prison walls. 9:35 a.m. Exercise period concludes for prisoners. 9:45 a.m. Prison officials notified Cavalcante is missing. 9:50 a.m. Prison is ordered into lockdown. 10:01 a.m. Chester County emergency services alerted, and escape siren sounded. 10:40 a.m. Chadds Ford Elementary School is notified of an escape.
August 31, 2023	Chester County Prison sergeant Jerry Beavers wrote to Cpt. Harry Griswold several hours after the escape. "He noted back in July that this inmate was planning an escape."
August 31, 2023	Cavalcante sighted about an hour after his escape walking 2 miles west of the prison.
September 1, 2023	Cavalcante breaks into the home of Ryan Drummond.
September 7, 2023	Cavalcante is sighted on Longwood Gardens' property.
September 7, 2023	Correctional officer on duty during the escape is fired.
September 9, 2023	Cavalcante steals a van from Baily's dairy farm.

September 9, 2023	Cavalcante seen at the home of a former coworker.
September 10, 2023	Cavalcante's sister Eleni Cavalcante is arrested by ICE officials for "immigration issues."
September 11, 2023	Cavalcante is placed on Interpol's Red Notice.
September 11, 2023	A 911 call is reported on a shooting near a South Coventry elementary school. Cavalcante breaks into a garage and steals a .22 rifle with scope and flashlight. Homeowner fires seven times at Cavalcante.
September 13, 2023	At 1:00 a.m., a DEA plane with thermal-imaging technology spots Cavalcante in the woods. Despite the sighting, police are forced to wait until sunrise to approach because of inclement weather, which hindered the surveillance plane from safely operating.
September 13, 2023	A police-trained Belgian Malinois named Yoda subdues Cavalcante by biting him on the head and holding on to him until police place Cavalcante into handcuffs.
September 13, 2023	Cavalcante is taken to Pennsylvania State Police barracks in Avondale and then transferred to State Correctional Institution Phoenix in Montgomery County.
September 18, 2023	County holds town meeting on escape.
November 10, 2023	Pennsylvania Attorney General's Office files charges of burglary, criminal trespassing, theft, and possession of a firearm against Cavalcante.
November 2023	Cavalcante is moved to SCI Greene in Waynesburg.
February 2, 2024	Cavalcante is held for trial on escape and related charges after a preliminary hearing in Kennett Square.
April 29, 2024	Holland is named warden of Chester County Prison.
May 6, 2024	Attorney Lonny Fish becomes Cavalcante's defense attorney.

APPENDIX B: CHESTER COUNTY PRISON HISTORY

Information from the Chester County government website, www.chesco.org

When Danilo Cavalcante scaled the walls of Chester County Prison in August 2024, he absconded from an institution housing prisoners since 1959.

Chester County Prison is located approximately 10 miles south of Chester County's seat, West Chester, Pennsylvania. The current prison was opened in 1959 and operated under the original construction until 1983, when parts of the prison underwent renovations and expansion, and in 1993 a new Pre-Release / Work Release Center was constructed on prison property. The current structure is one of only four such buildings used as the county jail since Chester County was incorporated by William Penn in 1682, as one of the three original counties. Chester County's first jail cells were built in 1786 and were located in the rear of the courthouse. Prior to 1786, the County House of Correction and Work-House was located in Chester, Pennsylvania (former county seat).

In 1839, the County of Chester built its first off-site jail at Market and New Streets in West Chester, Pennsylvania. This structure subsequently underwent alteration and additions up until 1941. This prison was modeled after the Walnut Street jail in Philadelphia, the first county institution, which was built in 1770. The only differences were the sanitary provisions, beds, and heating for each cell.

In July 1951, the County of Chester realized that major steps were needed to correct some of the worn-out features in the 1839 jail. After an extensive survey of the building by architects, it was established that the building was in poor condition and was declared unsafe by the Department of Labor and Industry. Architects were then asked to provide alternatives to the county commissioners to make some kind of future projection for the renewal of the county jail. The county commissioners explored prisoner population growth, site locations, and costs during the years 1952 through 1954.

In 1954, pressure intensified when grand juries called on some kind of action to be taken on the part of Chester County to rectify the unsafe conditions at its jail. During the studies between 1952 through 1954, it was determined that remodeling or rebuilding in the heart of West Chester was not justifiable due to lack of space. The county commissioners formed a committee in November 1954 to make a survey of alternative locations for the new jail. In May 1955 the committee recommended that the new prison be constructed on land owned by the County Institutional District adjacent to the County Home in Pocopson, with the intent of developing a prison farm. In the fall of 1955, extensive studies were conducted to determine if the property would be adequate to support such a facility. The studies also included research on preliminary plans and specifications for a new prison.

In February 1956, the architects reported to the commissioners on the recommendations for the capacity of the new prison. These recommendations were in accordance with a study projecting the growth of the county up until the year 1965. The recommended prison capacity was a figure of 142 individual cells. These cells were broken down into seventy-two minimum-security cells, forty-eight medium-security cells, ten maximum-security cells, and twelve female cells, for a total prisoner capacity of the recommended 142. The recommendations made by the architects to the commissioners were viewed by the judges as being ultraconservative. They felt that if proper security facilities were provided in the new prison, many of those prisoners previously sentenced to the state penitentiary would be sentenced to the county prison. The commissioners further decided that the assumption of 1965, as the point of saturation populationwise, was working too close for comfort. They suggested that the population figure be extended to 1970. The commissioners also took into account the modern train of thought that insisted upon rehabilitation programs for the prisoners that would provide classrooms for academic education, shops for vocational training, and facilities for psychiatric analysis and therapy. The county commissioners had to determine what would be considered reasonable and reachable for a county jail. They also had to distinguish a clear division that would decide the responsibilities of a county prison versus a state penitentiary. It was determined that the length of sentence would decide what was reasonable for the county jail and its role and responsibility in such programs. The commissioners therefore decided that the twenty-three-month sentence, which often was commuted to something less, would become the pivotal point short of which an extensive rehabilitative program would not be necessary. Although various aspects of this subject were explored, it was determined that the new county prison would have shops and facilities for rug weaving, chair caning, and similar simple occupations, along with the operation of the kitchen, cannery, laundry, and maintenance services around the prison, for those prisoners not fitted or adjusted to work on the farm or throughout the community. This policy would, with certain exception, prevent the gradual glutting of large segments of cells with a rigid population of long-term prisoners for which it is not intended or equipped.

The concern and reluctance both of the commissioners and architects was not to overbuild the prison facilities, but they were appreciative of the foresight expressed by the judges in their insistence upon the general increase in the number of cells needed. It was decided that the boiler room, kitchen, dining room, etc. were to be built adequately so that they could handle future expansion. It was also decided that the term "minimum security" was to be dropped because it was equated with dormitory living areas and, for the times, this was not condoned by the Pennsylvania penal code.

This all led to the cells being designed for individual confinement with the exception of the infirmary ward. Therefore, the term "medium and maximum security" was adopted for Chester County Farms.

The prison comprised two basic cell types. The first was the maximum-security unit, which was built with two rows of cells back to back, with an access chase to the plumbing between the two rows. The two rows would have separate corridors so that the prisoners cannot see or communicate with each other. The windows for the wing would be high up in the exterior wall, away from the cells and on the level of the upper tier. The second type was the medium-security wings, which were to have a central corridor with the cells on both sides facing each other and with security windows in each cell on the outside walls.

The scheduled construction of the 1959 prison comprised 128 medium-security cells, twenty-four maximum-security cells, fifteen female cells, and four juvenile cells, for a total population of 171 individual cells. In addition to the general population cells, there were two restraint cells and two treatment cells in the maximum-security unit for men. There were also plans for one restraint cell and one treatment cell for women. The prison also had four single cells and a large holding cell in connection with the admissions area, as well as plans for a five-to-six-bed infirmary for men and a two-to-three-bed infirmary for women. These plans were approved by the judges as minimum requirements, and that only because of the flexibility of the plan to support future expansion. The county commissioners also approved the program along with the preliminary plans, outlined specifications, and the budget for the new prison after the presentation of the Citizens Prison Survey Committee, the Pennsylvania Prison Society, the Prison Board, and the Commissioners of Corrections of the Commonwealth of Pennsylvania. The architects then were authorized to proceed with the contract drawings and specifications. The dedication of the 1959 prison was conducted on January 14, 1959, at 2:00 p.m., and it has subsequently been in operation ever since."

INDEX